EAST·WEST

STUDENT BOOK 1

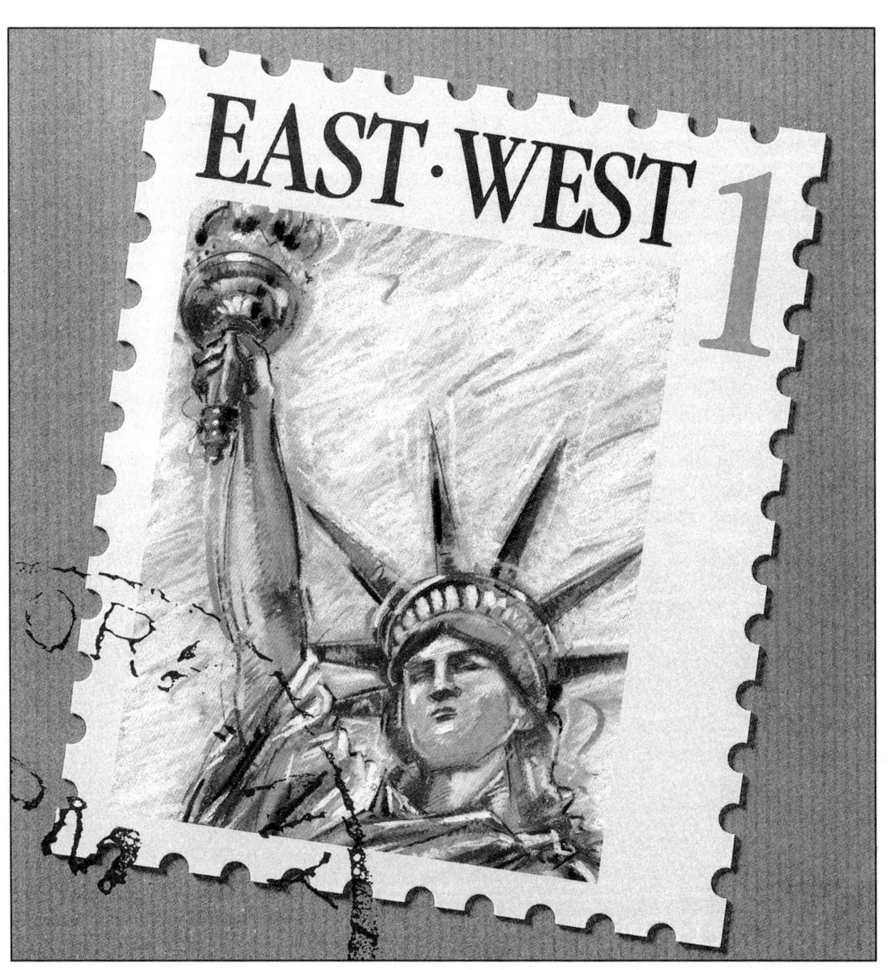

by Kathleen Graves and David P. Rein

Oxford University Press
1988

Oxford University Press

200 Madison Avenue
New York, NY 10016 USA

Walton Street
Oxford OX2 6DP England

Oxford is a trademark of Oxford University Press.

Library of Congress Cataloging-in-Publication Data

Graves, Kathleen.
East–West / Kathleen Graves, David P. Rein.
p. cm.
ISBN 0-19-434241-7
1. English language—Textbooks for foreign speakers.
I. Rein, David P. II. Title.
PE1128.G654 1988
428.2'4—dc19 88-17821
CIP

Developmental Editor: Susan Lanzano
Assistant Editor: Jeannie Rabenda
Editorial Assistant: Mary Sutherland
Art Director: Shireen Nathoo
Arts Researcher: Paula Radding

Illustrations by:
Lisa Adams, Rowan Barnes-Murphey (represented by Evelyne Johnson), Bryan Haynes, Marie-Helene Jeeves, Maggie Ling, Barbara Maslen, Robbie Marantz, Jacqui Morgan, Anna Rich, Mark Rowney, Joseph Shea, Debra Solomon, and Anna Veltfórt.

Studio and location photography by:
Richard Haynes, Paul Chakmakjian

The publishers would like to thank the following for permission to reproduce photographs:
E. Adams/Gamma-Liaison; Stan Barouh/JVC Jazz Festival New York; The Bettmann Archive; M. Biggins/Gamma-Liaison; Brazilian Tourism Foundation; British Tourist Authority; Larry Chiger/Four By Five; Ginger Chih/Peter Arnold, Inc.; Ray Ellis/Photo Researchers, Inc.; Eunice Harris/Photo Researchers,Inc.; Harry Hartman/Bruce Coleman, Inc.; Dan Helms/Duomo; Italian Government Travel Office; Japan National Tourist Organization; Mark Keller/Four By Five; A. Knudsen/Sygma; Kodansha International; B. Lacombe/Gamma-Liaison; J.J. Lapeyronnie/Gamma-Liaison; Robert Llewellyn/Four By Five; David J. Maenza/Image Bank; Benn Mitchell/Image Bank; Hanae Mori USA, Inc.; Jeffry Myers/Four By Five; Bradley Olman/Bruce Coleman, Inc.; Phototeque; J. Rozsa/Gamma-Liaison; P.A. Savoie/Bruce Coleman, Inc.; S. Schapiro/Gamma-Liaison; S. Schapiro/Sygma; Martha Swope; Norman Owen Tomalin/Bruce Coleman, Inc.; J. Travert/Gamma-Liaison; Turner Entertainment Co.; Universal Pictures; UPI/Bettmann Newsphotos; Alvis Upitis/Image Bank; Warner Brothers

Graphics by:
Maj Britt Hagsted, Oxford University Press Technical Graphics Department

Additional thanks for providing printed pieces for reproduction:
Capital Sports; Carnegie Hall Archives; James F. O'Leary, General Manager, MBTA; Mike Quon

Cover illustration by Barbara Maslen, photograph by Carl Steinbrenner.

Special thanks to Nancy Haffner, Stylist; Sally Foord-Kelcey, Art Editor, OUP Britain; Denise Johnson, Photo Researcher; April Okano, Designer

Printing (last digit): 10 9 8 7 6 5

Printed in Hong Kong.

Acknowledgements

The authors and publisher would like to thank the following people for reviewing *East West 1* and providing helpful comments and suggestions: Edwin Aloiau and Dirk Binder, Tokyo Foreign Language College; Torkil Christensen, Hokusei Junior College, Sapporo; Thomas Clark, ELEC, Toyko; Rosa Erlichman, União Cultural Brasil-Estados Unidos, São Paolo; Donald Freeman, The School for International Training, Brattleboro, Vermont; Barbara Fujiwara, Doshisha Women's Junior College, Kyoto; Donald Occhiuzzo and Kathy Harrington, Associação Alumni, São Paolo; Rick Shelly, JAL Coordination Services Co. Ltd., Tokyo; Paul Thompson, Seinan Gakuin University, Fukuoka; and the students in the authors' English Structures classes in the M.A.T. program at the School for International Training, Brattleboro, Vermont.

To the Student

Welcome to EAST WEST. As you use this book, please remember:

When you work with a partner, always take turns as Student A and Student B.

When you do information gap exercises like the one on page 12, cover your partner's side with the blue mask inside this book.

Use English when you speak to your teacher and classmates. Here are some expressions that will be useful to you both in and outside of class.

We hope you enjoy EAST WEST.

Contents

UNIT 1

Andrew: Excuse me, do you speak English?
Kenichi: Yes, I do, a little.
Andrew: Great! Could we borrow your map?
Kenichi: Sure. Here it is.
Andrew: Thank you.

Andrew: Where are you from?
Kenichi: I'm Japanese, from Osaka. What about you? Are you from the States?
Laura: Yes, we are. Are you in Paris on vacation?
Kenichi: No, I'm studying French.
Andrew: Really? What do you do?
Kenichi: I'm a fashion designer.
Laura: Well, it's a small world! I'm a fashion designer, too!
Andrew: By the way, I'm Andrew Scott, and this is my wife, Laura.
Kenichi: My name's Kenichi Nakano. How do you do?

Speaking

1

Fill in the verbs. Use *are/ 're* or *is/ 's.* Then match questions with answers.

1. Where .... Laura and Andrew Scott from?
2. .... Kenichi Nakano in Paris on vacation?
3. .... Andrew and Laura American?
4. Where .... Laura, Andrew and Kenichi?
5. .... Laura an actress?
6. Where'.......... Kenichi from?
7. .... Andrew and Laura from France?
8. .... Kenichi a fashion designer?

a. No, she ....n't.
b. Yes, they ....
c. He'.......... Japanese.
d. Yes, he ....
e. No, he ....n't.
f. No, they ....n't.
g. They'.................... in Paris.
h. They'.......... from the United States.

2

A, ask B the questions in Exercise 1 in any order. **B**, listen carefully to A's questions. Answer them.

A: Where are Laura, Andrew and Kenichi?
B: They're in Paris.

3

A, ask B questions. **B**, you're Kenichi Nakano. Answer A's questions.

. . . *English?*

A: Do you speak English?
B: Yes, I do, a little.

1. . . . English?
2. . . . map?
3. . . . from?
4. . . . on vacation?
5. . . . do?

4

A, ask B for a pen and a dictionary. **B**, ask A for a pencil and an English book. Have conversations like these:

A: Excuse me, could I borrow your ____________?
B: Sure. Here it is.
A: Thank you.
B: You're welcome.

OR

A: Excuse me, could I borrow your ____________?
B: I need it right now. I'm sorry.
A: That's OK.

5

Pronunciation

At the end of a *yes/no* question, your voice goes up: Do you speak French?

At the end of an information question, your voice goes down: Where's Brasilia?

Practice asking and answering questions like these:

A: Do you speak French?
B: Yes, I do.
OR No, I don't.

A: Where's Brasilia?
B: It's in Brazil.
OR I don't know.

Languages	Capital cities	Countries
Arabic	Brasilia	The United States
English	Cairo	Canada
French	Moscow	Egypt
Italian	Ottawa	France
Japanese	Paris	Italy
Portuguese	Rome	Japan
Russian	Tokyo	The Soviet Union
Chinese	Washington, D.C.	Brazil
____________	____________	____________
	____________	____________

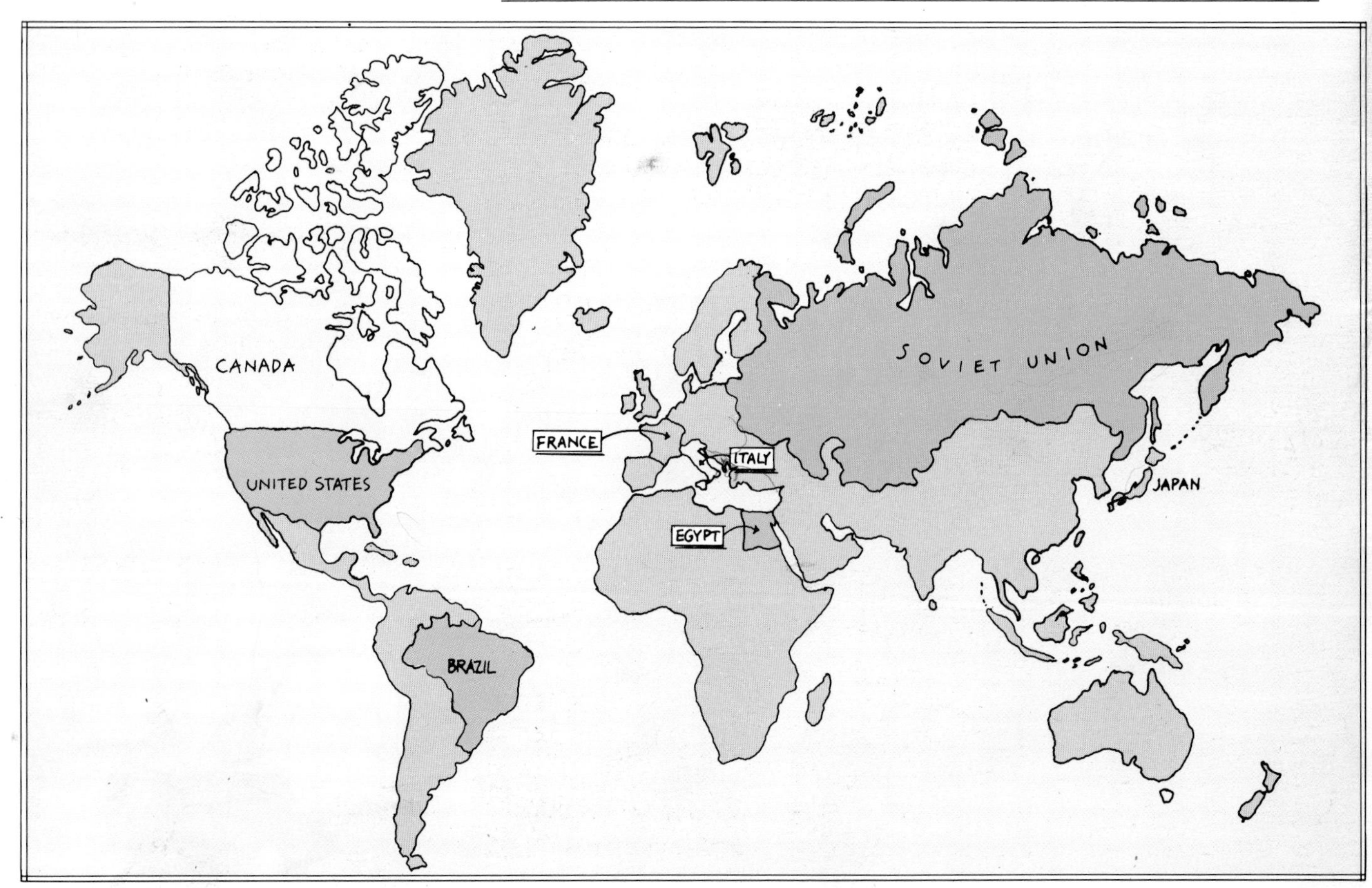

6

Make true and false statements about the famous people in the pictures. Use *a* or *an*. For example, *a politician, an actress.*

A: Brooke Shields is American.
B: That's right.
C: She's a businesswoman.
D: That isn't right. She's an actress.

Names	Countries	Professions
Harold Robbins	The United States	writer
Catherine Deneuve	France	businesswoman/actress
Brooke Shields	The United States	actress
Hanae Mori	Japan	fashion designer
Diana Ross	The United States	actress/singer
Pierre Cardin	France	fashion designer
Gloria Vanderbilt	The United States	businesswoman
Yasushi Inoue	Japan	writer

Gloria Vanderbilt

Yasushi Inoue

Brooke Shields

Hanae Mori

Catherine Deneuve

Harold Robbins

Diana Ross

Pierre Cardin

7

A, ask questions about these famous people. **B**, close your book and answer the questions.

A: Where's Harold Robbins from?
B: The United States.
OR He's American.

A: What does Pierre Cardin do?
B: He's a fashion designer.

8

Work in groups of four. **A**, you're a famous person. **B**, **C**, **D**, guess A's name.

B: Are you American?
A: No, I'm not.
C: Are you from France?
A: Yes, I am.
D: Are you a businesswoman?
A: No, I'm not.
C: You're Pierre Cardin.
A: That's right!

9

A and **B**, you're famous people. Ask each other questions.

A: Where .... from?
B: .... What about you?
A: .... (too!)
B: What do you do?
A: I'm .... What about you?
B: .... (too!) By the way, I'm ....
A: My name's .... How do you do?

10

Culture Capsule

These people are meeting for the first time.

They're shaking hands.

They're bowing.

What do people do in your country?

11

Repeat the conversation in Exercise 9. This time give true information about yourself.

Nationalities	**Occupations**
Brazilian	teacher
Italian	student
Russian	writer
Egyptian	photographer
Spanish	actor
Chinese	doctor
Mexican	....
....	....

12

Two pairs get together. Introduce yourself and your partner.

I'm *(name)* I'm a/an *(occupation)* I'm from *(place)* This is *(name)* He's/She's a/an *(occupation)* (too). He's/She's from *(place)* (too).

13

Put It Together

- Choose two new nationalities, occupations and names for yourself.

Country/nationality	**Occupation**	**Name**
1.	....	....
2.	....	....

- You're in Toronto, Canada. You're waiting for a bus to Ottawa. Start a conversation with your partner. Ask to borrow something. Then introduce yourself and find out about your partner.

In Conversation 1, **A**, you want to borrow B's bus schedule.
In Conversation 2, **B**, you want to borrow A's newspaper.

I know how to . . .

USE THESE FORMS

☐ **Subject Pronouns**

I, he, she, it, you, we, they

☐ **Present Tense of Be**

I	am ('m)	I'm	not
he she it	is ('s)	he she it	is not (isn't)
you we they	are ('re)	you we they	are not (aren't)

questions

Is he American? Where's he from?

short answers

Yes, he is. No, he isn't.

statements

This is Billy Joel. He's a singer.
He isn't a fashion designer.

☐ **A/An**

He's	a	teacher doctor
	an	eye doctor actor

USE ENGLISH TO

☐ **get someone's attention**
Excuse me.

☐ **ask to borrow something**
Could I/we borrow your map?
Sure.

☐ **show interest**
Really?

☐ **introduce myself**
I'm Andrew Scott./My name's Kenichi Nakano.

☐ **introduce someone else**
This is my wife, Laura.

☐ **greet someone new**
How do you do?

☐ **give and accept thanks**
Thank you.
You're welcome.

☐ **ask and answer these questions**
Do you speak English?
Where are you from?
What do you do?

☐ **talk about these subjects**
names countries nationalities occupations

☐ UNDERSTAND THESE EXPRESSIONS

Great!
By the way, . . .
That's right/wrong.
What about you?
It's a small world.
be on vacation
shake hands

CHECKLIST

Listening

1

Complete these conversations. (Circle *a* or *b*).

1. a. No, I'm not.
   b. Yes, I do, a little.
2. a. Thank you.
   b. Sure. Here it is.
3. a. That's OK.
   b. Thank you.
4. a. I'm a writer.
   b. I'm Mexican, from Cuernavaca.
5. a. No, I'm studying English.
   b. No, I'm here on vacation.
6. a. Really? What do you do?
   b. Yes, we are.
7. a. I'm a teacher.
   b. I'm studying Italian.
8. a. What about you?
   b. How do you do? I'm Koji Asaba.

2

Listen to each question and answer about the famous people in this unit. Mark the answers *T* (true) or *F* (false).

1. ___ 4. ___ 7. ___
2. ___ 5. ___ 8. ___
3. ___ 6. ___

3

Margaret Winters is an English teacher. She and a friend are looking at this picture of Margaret's class. Fill in the countries and the occupations, using the information below.

Brazil	Italy	actor	singer
Canada	Japan	designer	teacher
Egypt	The Soviet Union	photographer	writer
France	The United States		

1. Akiko ....
2. Christophe ....
3. Sami ....
4. Maria ....

4

Give true answers.

1. ....
2. ....
3. ....
4. ....
5. ....
6. ....

MOON
OF INDIA
"MOON OF INDIA"
IS MISSING
New York: The famous "Moon of India" necklace is missing from the City Museum. According to Alexander Gray, museum director, the necklace. . .

Episode One

It is April 17. Alexander Gray, the director of the City Museum, is talking to newspaper reporters. "This is a terrible loss for the museum. The Moon of India is a very important necklace."

"How much is it worth?"

"More than four million dollars."

"Mr. Gray, are there any suspects?"

"Not yet. But the police are working on it day and night."

"Do you think the thief is somebody from the museum?"

"The police are looking at all the information we have. That's all. Thank you."

A man is walking along a street at night. He is worried and looks behind him. He goes into a phone booth and calls the police. Officer Casey answers the phone and hears something very strange: "I know about the Moon of India."

Casey says, "The Moon of India? Really?"

"The necklace from the museum. Please, I don't have much time."

"Okay. What's your name?"

"Richardson, Paul Richardson."

"Okay, what do you know about the necklace?"

"My partner and I took it. But now he's gone."

"Where is he?"

There is a gun shot. Richardson tries to talk, "Venice . . . the Princess . . . ."

Casey repeats, "Venice? Princess? What about them?"

Richardson is silent.

"Richardson. Richardson, are you there?"

Officer Casey is reporting to Police Lieutenant Washington; "One suspect, Paul Richardson, 48, is dead. His partner is gone."

"Maybe his partner took the necklace and then killed Richardson."

"Maybe. What about Richardson's last words—'Venice . . . Princess . . . .' What do they mean?"

"The partner is going to Venice with a princess? Or a princess is in Venice? Is there a Princess Hotel in Venice?"

"Maybe it's a ship." Lieutenant Washington looks in the newspaper at ships' schedules and sees that a ship called 'The Princess' leaves Venice on April 21.

"Okay, get a list of people on the Princess. We're going to put a police officer on that ship."

Comprehension Check

1. What is the Moon of India and why is it important?
2. Does Alexander Gray know who took the Moon of India?
3. Who are Alexander Gray, Paul Richardson, Officer Casey and Lt. Washington?
4. Why did Paul Richardson call the police?
5. Who probably shot Paul Richardson?
6. What is the meaning of "Venice . . . Princess"?

UNIT 2

Announcer: Ladies and gentlemen, the Incredible Zarkov, mind reader!
Zarkov: Thank you. . . . I see some letters. The first letter is a *C*. There's an *L*, too, and an *E*. No, that's wrong. There isn't an *E*. I see an *O*, an *R* and an *A*. *C-L-O-R-A*?
Woman: Is it my name?
Zarkov: What's your name, please?
Woman: Carol.
Zarkov: And you spell it *C-A-R-O-L*, right?
Woman: That's right!

Zarkov: Now I see some numbers. There's a *7*. There are two *9*s, and there's an *11*. Tell me, Carol, what's your address?
Woman: 799 11th Street! That's incredible!
Zarkov: Are there apartments in that building, Carol? Is there one on the second floor? Is that your apartment?
Woman: Yes! Yes! How many rooms are there?

Zarkov: Three. I see the living room. There're two windows. There's a green sofa in front of the windows. There's a chair across from the sofa. It's an easy chair. There's a door to the right, and there's a bookcase next to it. There're some plants in the bookcase, but there aren't any books.
Woman: That's right!

Zarkov: This is very strange. There's a bed in the living room, and there isn't any furniture in the bedroom. Hmm. Are you painting your bedroom, Carol?
Woman: Yes! Zarkov, you're incredible!

Speaking

1

Identify these objects by their numbers:

floor lamp	dresser	curtains
telephone	books	mirror
coffee table	easy chair	end table
table lamp	pictures	bed

A: What's number one?
B: A mirror.
A: What's number four?
B: An end table.
A: What's number two?
B: Curtains.

2

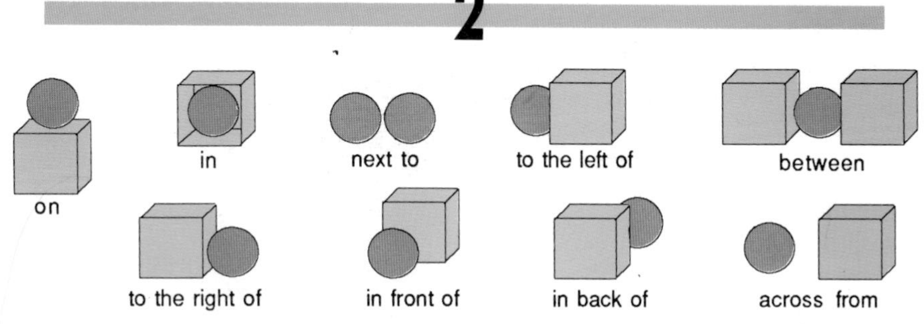

Talk about the locations of the objects in Carol's living room. Use these phrases:

on the window/end table/coffee table
between the windows
to the right/left of the sofa
in front of/across from the sofa

A: Is there a floor lamp in the living room?
B: Yes, there's one to the left of the sofa. Are there any books?
A: Yes, there are some on the coffee table.

3

• Fill in the missing ordinal numbers. Then practice saying them.

1	first (1st)	9	ninth (9th)
2	....	10	....
3	third (3rd)	11	....
4	fourth (4th)	12	twelfth (12th)
5	fifth (5th)	13	thirteenth (13th)
6	....	14	....
7	....	15	fifteenth (15th)
8	....		last

• Review the alphabet in English. Then ask and answer questions about the letters in REMEMBERED.

A: What's the eighth letter?
B: The eighth letter is an *R*.

4

What's My Word?

A, think of a word. **B**, give letters to guess the word.

(A's word is *please*.)
B: How many letters are there in your word?
A: Six.

___ ___ ___ ___ ___ ___

B: Are there any Es?
A: Yes, there are two. The third letter and the sixth letter are Es.

___ ___ e ___ ___ e

B: Are there any Ts?
A: No, there aren't.

___ ___ e ___ ___ e

B: Is there a P?
A: Yes, there's one. It's the first letter.

p ___ e ___ ___ e

B: Is the word "please"?
A: Yes, that's right.

p l e a s e

5

Pronunciation

Practice saying these addresses:

200 Woodland Street (St.)	Two hundred Woodland Street
409 Fuller Avenue (Ave.)	Four oh nine Fuller Avenue
799 11th St.	Seven ninety nine Eleventh Street
1712 Park Road (Rd.)	Seventeen twelve Park Road

555 Highland Ave.
1987 East Rd.
206 Green St.

6

• Choose a first name, last name and address.

Carol McMann
100 East Main St.

Anne	Cline, Klein	19 Amherst Rd.
Carol	Conn, Kahn	100 East Main St.
Larry	Haines, Haynes	315 Elm St.
Mark	McMahan, McMann	802 Lake Rd.
Roy	Reilly, Riley	6876 University Ave.

• Practice this conversation:

A: What's your name, please?
B: Carol McMann.
A: How do you spell your last name?
B: M-C, capital M-A-N-N.
A: And what's your address?
B: 100 East Main Street.

• Practice the conversation again. Give true answers.

7

Pronunciation

Some nouns add an **s** or a **z** sound for the plural. Others add an **əz** sound for the plural. Practice saying these words.

/**s**/	/**z**/	/**əz**/
lamps	chairs	bookcases
plants	doors	boxes of books
desks	pictures	paintbrushes
....	windows	pieces of chalk
....	....	....

Ask and answer questions about your classroom.

A: Are there any pictures in the classroom?
B: Yes, there's one. OR No, there aren't.

 8

 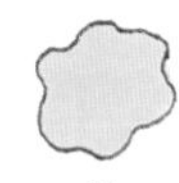 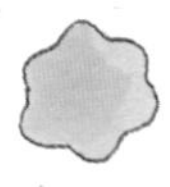 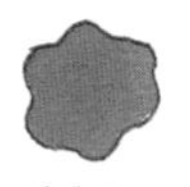  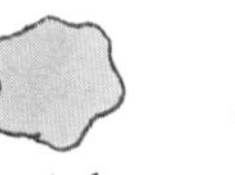    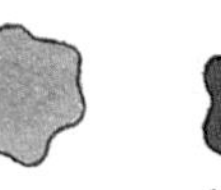 

red orange yellow green blue purple pink black white gray brown

You and your partner have different pictures of the same room.
Cover your partner's side of the page. Ask about the furniture in his/her room.

bookcase floor lamp end table table lamp coffee table sofa easy chair telephone

A

1. Ask about your list of furniture. Check the correct ones.

   A: Is there an orange bookcase in the room?
   B: No, there isn't.
   A: Is there a gray bookcase in the room?
   B: Yes, there is.

2. Answer your partner's questions about your picture.

3. Ask your partner where things are. Draw them in your picture.

   A: Where's the gray bookcase?
   B: It's next to the floor lamp.

B

1. Answer your partner's questions about your picture.

   A: Is there an orange bookcase in the room?
   B: No, there isn't.
   A: Is there a gray bookcase in the room?
   B: Yes, there is.

2. Ask about your list. Check the correct ones.

3. Ask your partner where things are. Draw them in your picture.

   A: Where's the gray bookcase?
   B: It's next to the floor lamp.

9
Culture Capsule

Some Americans live in houses. Some Americans live in apartments. In an apartment, there are usually one or two bedrooms, a kitchen, a bathroom and a living room. Sometimes there's a dining room.

Think of an apartment in your country. How many rooms are there? What are they? Is there usually a lot of furniture in the living room?

Do you live in an apartment? Do you live in a house? Describe your living room.

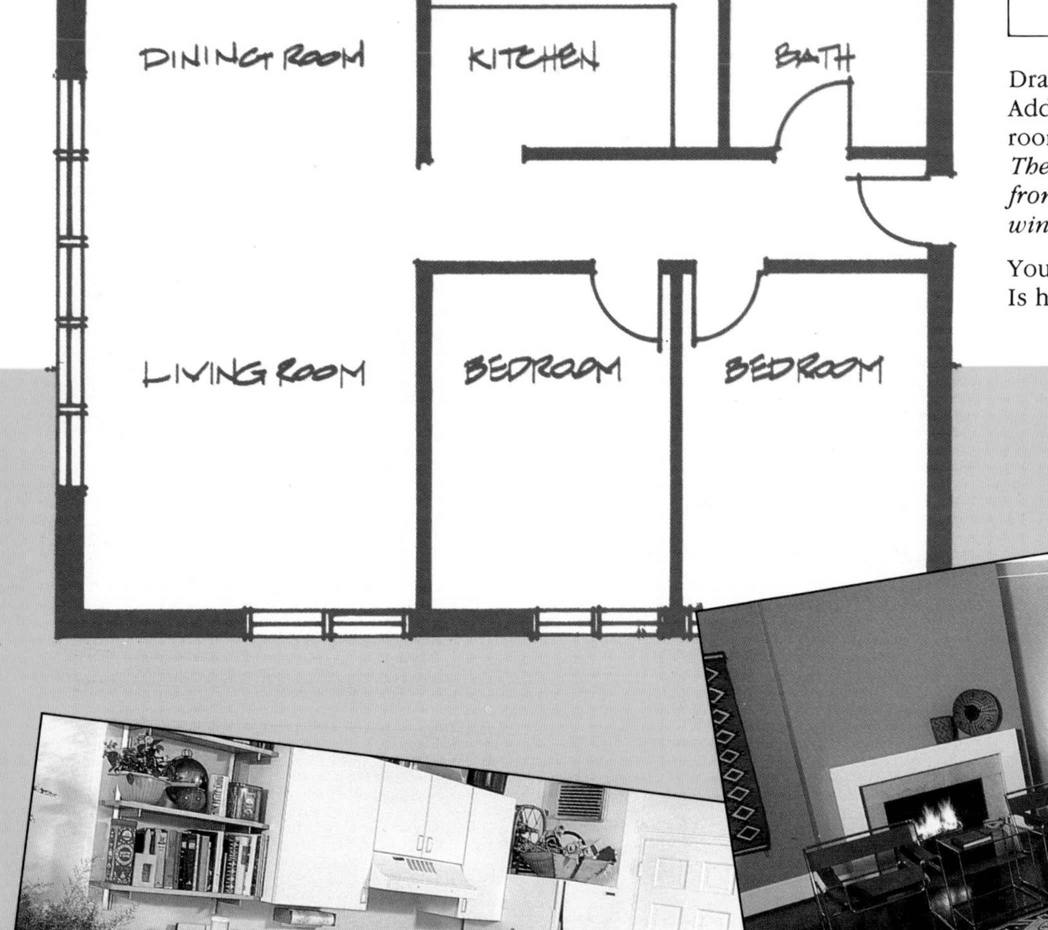

10
Put It Together

This is an empty living room. There are three windows.

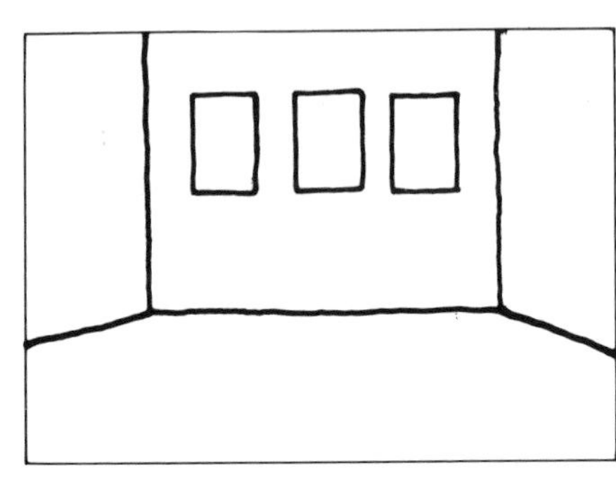

Draw this room on a piece of paper. Add furniture. Describe the living room to your partner. For example: *There's a sofa. It's brown. It's in front of the first and second windows. . . .*

Your partner draws the living room. Is his/her picture right or wrong?

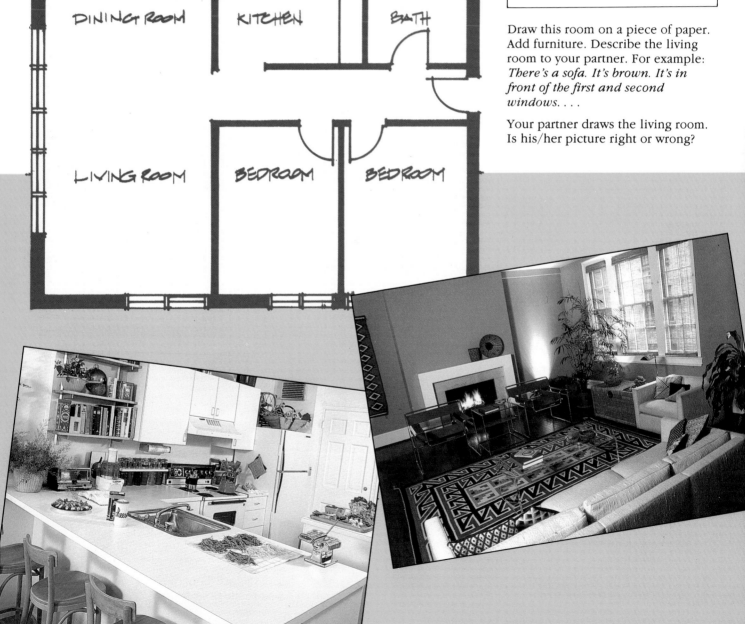

I know how to . . .

CHECKLIST

USE THESE FORMS

☐ **There is/are**

questions

Is / Are	there	a lamp / any lamps	in the room?
Is	there	a lamp	in the room?
Are		any lamps	

short answers

Yes, there | is. / are.
No, there | isn't. / aren't.

statements

There	's a		lamp	on the table.
	are	two / some	lamps	
	aren't	any	lamps	

☐ **One/Some/Any**

questions

Are there any books in the room?

statements

There | 's one / are some (books) / aren't any (books) | in the bookcase.

☐ **A/An - The**

There's *an end table* and *a lamp* next to the sofa.
The end table is green and *the lamp* is white.

☐ **Noun Plurals**

/s/	/z/	/əz/
lamps	chairs	bookcases
desk	windows	boxes

☐ **Prepositions of Place**

in on between to the right/left of
in front of across from next to

☐ **Ordinal Numbers**

1st first	5th fifth	9th ninth	13th thirteenth	21st twenty-first
2nd second	6th sixth	10th tenth	14th fourteenth	22nd twenty-second
3rd third	7th seventh	11th eleventh	15th fifteenth	23rd twenty-third
4th fourth	8th eighth	12th twelfth	20th twentieth	25th twenty-fifth

USE ENGLISH TO

☐ **ask for someone's name and address**
What's your name (please)?
Carol McMann.
What's your address?
100 East Main Street.

☐ **ask how to spell something**
How do you spell your last name?
M-C, capital M-A-N-N.

☐ **describe a room**
The living room has two windows.
There's a sofa in front of the windows. . . .

☐ **talk about these subjects**
colors, furniture, rooms of a house, addresses, numbers

☐ UNDERSTAND THESE EXPRESSIONS

Ladies and gentlemen   Thank you.   That's incredible.

Listening

1

Anne is taking people's names and addresses.

Part 1: Listen for the spelling of each person's name. Circle the correct letter.

1. Frank's last name is
   a. Gillmore.
   b. Gilmore.
   c. Gilmour.
2. Ray's last name is
   a. Braun.
   b. Brown.
   c. Browne.
3. Ingrid's last name is
   a. Andersen.
   b. Anderson.
   c. Andresen.
4. Rich's last name is
   a. Reade.
   b. Read.
   c. Reid.
5. Pat's last name is
   a. MacLeod.
   b. McCloud.
   c. McLeod.
6. Doris's last name is
   a. Wait.
   b. Waite.
   c. Waitt.

Part 2: Listen again to the conversations and fill in the street number in each person's address.

1. (Frank) .... Harris Ave.
2. (Ray) .... Green Street
3. (Ingrid) .... Hill Road
4. (Rich) .... Belmont Avenue
5. (Pat) .... Williams Road
6. (Doris) .... High Street

2

Gail and Manuel are playing *What's My Word?* Fill in the correct letters as you hear them.

___	___	___	___	___	___	___	___	___	___
1	2	3	4	5	6	7	8	9	10

3

Sandy wants to take a picture of some people in her office. Find the people in the picture. Write their numbers below their names.

Janice	Allen	Howard	Doug	Diane	Rosa	Kristin	Sandy
....	....	....	....	....	....	....	....

4

Give true answers.

1. ....
2. ....
3. ....
4. ....

Episode Two

It is April 21. In Venice passengers are boarding the *Princess.* People are carrying flowers and luggage. A man in a white uniform, the purser, is giving directions and information.

"I'm Christina Jordan and this is my aunt, Agatha Jordan," says one of the passengers to the purser.

The Purser looks at a list: "Welcome aboard. Jordan. . . . Yes, here you are. Cabin 30, that's on B deck. There's an elevator over there."

"Thank you."

The *Princess* is leaving Venice. People are calling out, "Goodbye! Bon voyage! Have a good trip!" and taking photographs. Christina is taking a photograph of Venice and a man walks in front of her camera. She photographs him by mistake.

"I'm very sorry, excuse me. I didn't see you," the man says.

"Don't worry, please. I have lots of film."

"Are you a photographer?"

"Oh no. It's only a hobby. I work for a museum in New York. My specialty is Egyptian art."

"Really? I like Egyptian art very much, especially the jewelry."

"And you?" asks Christina. "What do you do?"

"Me? A little of this and a little of that. I'm Frank Adams. Glad to meet you."

"My name's Christina Jordan. How do you do?"

A bell rings.

"It's time for lunch. I'm hungry. Where's your table?" Frank asks.

"We're at Table 5."

"Oh, you and your husband?"

"No, I'm with my aunt."

"Really? I'm at Table 5, too. After you, Miss Jordan."

"Please call me Christina."

After lunch, Christina returns to her cabin where her aunt is resting.

"How are you feeling, Aunt Agatha?"

"Just fine, dear. Now where are my glasses?"

"You're wearing them, Aunt Agatha!"

"Why yes, I am, I'm so forgetful! Did you have lunch?"

"Yes. It's two thirty."

"Are there any interesting people at our table, Christina dear?"

"Well, yes, there are. There's Frank Adams. He's the one who walked in front of my camera today. He's really very nice. There's Robert Grant.... He's very handsome. And there's Lucy Cardozo. She's from New York."

"Well, dear," says Aunt Agatha. "I think dinner at Table 5 is going to be very interesting."

Comprehension Check

1. What do you know about Christina Jordan?
2. Who is Frank Adams? How does he meet Christina?
3. What do you know about Agatha Jordan?
4. Who ate lunch at Table 5?

UNIT 3

At the Miami Health Institute, Miami, Florida

Nan: Hi, Jon. How's it going?
Jon: OK. Thanks, Nan.
Nan: Dr. Hummel, I'd like you to meet Jonathan Wilkins. Jon, this is Dr. Paul Hummel. He's from Switzerland.
Dr. Hummel: How do you do, Mr. Wilkins?
Jon: Hello, Dr. Hummel. It's nice to meet you.
Nan: Jon writes our newsletter, Dr. Hummel. He'd like to interview you.
Dr. Hummel: Certainly.
Nan: Well, I'd better get back to work. Goodbye for now, Dr. Hummel. See you later, Jon.

Jon: Where do you work, Dr. Hummel?
Dr. Hummel: At the Eisen Company, in Basel. We make medical supplies.
Jon: Oh, and what exactly do you do there?
Dr. Hummel: I'm in charge of the research department.
Jon: Do you live in Basel, too?
Dr. Hummel: No, I don't. I live in a small town near the city.
Jon: Do you have a family?
Dr. Hummel: Yes, I do. My wife's also a chemist. She works at the same company. We have two sons. They're both in school.
Jon: How old are they?
Dr. Hummel: Twelve and seventeen.
Jon: Do they want to be chemists, too?
Dr. Hummel: Well, the older one does, but the younger one doesn't. Right now he wants to be a rock singer. Who knows? He changes his mind every day.

MHI Newsletter, No. 5

WELCOME, INTERNATIONAL VISITORS!

MIAMI, July 19. This week we have five visitors from other countries. When you see them, please say hello and welcome them to MHI.

Dr. Paul Hummel is in charge of the research department at the Eisen Company in Basel, Switzerland. He, his wife, Anna, and their two sons live near Basel. Dr. Hummel and his wife are both chemists.

Mr. and Mrs. James Richards are computer programmers from Sydney, Australia. They both work at Drew Laboratories there. They live in an apartment near a beach. Jim says, "We don't have any children, but Carole's younger brother lives with us. He's a good kid." Carole agrees.

Felicidad Diaz comes to us from Mexico. She teaches at ABC Hospital in Mexico City. Ms. Diaz is single. She lives at home with her parents, an older brother and a younger sister. Her name means "happiness" in Spanish, and she is a happy person.

Speaking

1

Complete these questions with *are, is, do* or *does.* Give short answers.

1. Where ....does.... Paul Hummel come from? ....Switzerland.....
2. Where .... Jon and Nan work? ....
3. Where .... MHI? ....
4. What .... the Eisen Company make? ....
5. How old .... Paul Hummel's sons? ....
6. Where .... Paul Hummel live? ....

2

Complete these questions with *do* or *does.* Give short answers with *do, does, don't* or *doesn't.*

1. ....Does.... Jon Wilkins write the newsletter? ....Yes, he does.....
2. .... Paul Hummel come from the United States? ....
3. .... his wife work at the Eisen Company? ....
4. .... the Hummels live in Basel? ....
5. .... their children go to school? ....
6. .... Dr. Hummel manage the research department? ....

3

- Ask and answer questions like the ones in Exercises 1 and 2.

A, ask about Mr. and Mrs. Richards. **B,** ask about Ms. Diaz.

- Ask and answer questions with *who.*

A: Who has two sons?
B: Paul Hummel (does). Who comes from Australia?
A: Carole and Jim Richards (do).

4

Practice the first conversation in this unit. There are three roles.

1. **A** and **B**, you work at MHI. B writes the newsletter. Use your real names. **C**, you're Mr. Richards (in Newsletter).
2. Practice the conversation again. (Switch roles.) This time C is Ms. Diaz.
3. This time C is Mrs. Richards.

5

Find out the missing information about the people in the chart.
Have conversations like this:

A: Where does Timothy work?
B: At Brown's Photo Studios.
A: Oh, that's right. He takes children's pictures.
B: Where do John and Jim work?

A

	Where do they work?	What do they do?
♂ Timothy		
♀ Jeanne	K-D Department Store	
♂ Dan		
♀ Lynn	home	
♀ Christina		
♂ John and ♂ Jim	The ABC Taxi Company	
♂ Tony and ♀ Marie		
♀ Lee	Sam's Used Cars	

design(s) jewelry

take(s) children's pictures

announce(s) the news

teach(es) Spanish

B

	Where do they work?	What do they do?
♂ John and ♂ Jim		
♀ Christina	Forrest University	
♀ Lynn		
♂ Timothy	Brown's Photo Studios	
♀ Lee		
♂ Tony and ♀ Marie	R and G Jewelry	
♀ Jeanne		
♂ Dan	WFBS Television	

manage(s) the sales department

sell(s) cars

drive(s) taxis

write(s) for a newspaper

6

Pronunciation

- A question with two choices sounds like this:

Do Dr. and Mrs. Martin Adams live on Guilford Street or Guilford Avenue?

- Practice saying these phrases. Notice how *in, on* and *at* are used for locations.

at	on	in
home 200 Woodland Street (number and street)	Woodland Street (street name only)	a house, an apartment, a room Miami (a city) Florida (a state, a prefecture) The United States (a country)

7

You're checking your company's mailing list. **A,** you have an old list. Ask B your questions. **B,** you have a new list. Give A the new information.

A

Street?

Adams, Dr. and Mrs. Martin – Guilford Avenue, Attleboro

A: Do Dr. and Mrs. Martin Adams live on Guilford Street or Guilford Avenue?

B: They live on Guilford Street.

1. Ask B your questions.

Street?

Adams, Dr. and Mrs. Martin – Guilford Avenue, Attleboro

12?

Albright, Mr.David – 9 Belmont Avenue Attleboro

Attleboro?

Amodeo, Deborah and John–377 Plain Road,South Attleboro

Place?

Audet, Louis – 18 Melrose Street, West Attleboro

2. You have a new list. Give B the correct information.

Macko, Gail and Arthur – 27 Canal Street, West Attleboro

Madden, Frank – Guilford

Makris, Paul and Cindy – 107 North Main Street, Vernon

Mauer, Norman R. – 30 Maple Street, Attleboro

B

Adams, Dr. and Mrs. Martin – Guilford Street, Attleboro

A: Do Dr. and Mrs. Martin Adams live on Guilford Street or Guilford Avenue?

B: They live on Guilford Street.

1. Give A the new information.

Adams, Dr. and Mrs. Martin – Guilford Street, Attleboro

Albright, Mr. David – 9 Belmont Avenue, Attleboro

Amodeo, Deborah and John – 377 Plain Road, South Attleboro

Audet, Louis – 18 Melrose Place, West Attleboro

2. You have an old list. Ask A your questions.

27?

Macko, Gail and Arthur – 25 Canal Street, West Attleboro

Madden, Frank – Guilford Attleboro?

North Main?

Makris, Paul and Cindy – 107 Main Street, Vernon

13?

Mauer, Norman R. – 30 Maple Street, Attleboro

8

Ask some classmates where they live, where they work and what they do.

• Talk to three other people in your class. Write down the answers.

A: Where do you live?
B: ....
A: (Where) do you work?
B: I work at .... OR I don't have a job.
A: What exactly do you do?

• Work with a partner. Tell your partner the names of the people you talked to. Ask each other about these people.

A: I talked to ...., ... and ....
B: Where does .... live?
A: ....

9

• Practice this conversation:

A: Do you have any brothers or sisters?
B: Yes, I do. I have an older sister and a younger brother.
OR No, I don't. I'm an only child.
A: What are their names?
B: My sister's name is Ruth. My brother's name is Tony.
A: Where do they live?
B: My sister lives in an apartment in New York. My brother lives at home.

• **A,** ask about B's family. **B,** give true answers. **A,** write down the information B gives you.

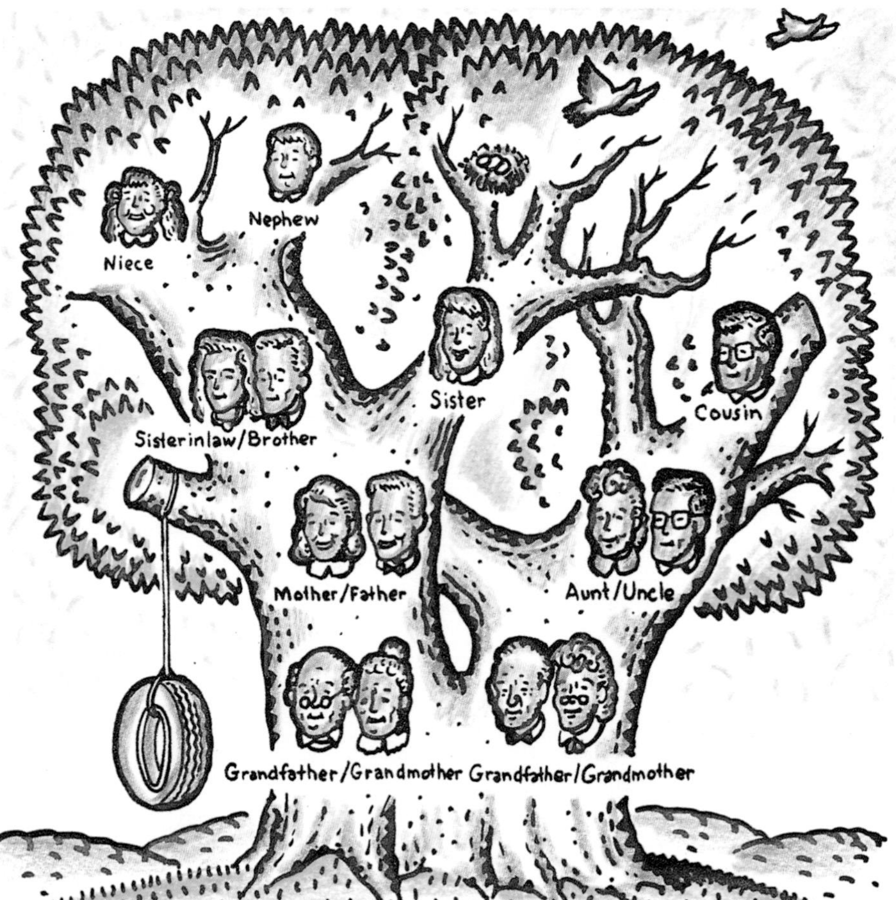

10

• Fill in the blanks and practice saying these words:

wife's = her
husband's = his
my wife's and my = our
son's = ...
sons' = ...
daughter's = ...
daughters' = ...

engaged	single	divorced
married	separated	widowed

• Practice this conversation:

A: Are you married?
B: Yes, I am. OR No, I'm not.
A: What's your wife's/husband's name?
B: Her/His name's Chris.
A: Do you have any children?
B: Yes, I/we do. I/we have two sons and a daughter. OR No, I/we don't.
A: What are their names?
B: Our sons' names are Matthew and John. Our daughter's name is Amy.
A: How old are they?
B: 13, 11 and 8.

• **A,** ask about B's family. **B,** give true answers. **A,** write down the information B gives you.

• Join another pair of students. Tell them what you know about your partner's family from this exercise and from Exercise 9.

11

Put It Together

Look at the family tree. Talk about your families.

A: Do you have any aunts and uncles?
B: Yes, I have two aunts and one uncle.
A: Where do they live?

I know how to . . .

USE THESE FORMS

☐ **Simple Present Tense**

I	work	he	works
you	do	she	does
we	have	it	has
they			

questions

(Where) Do you / Does he | work?

short answers

Yes, | I do. / he does.   No, | I don't. / he doesn't.

statements

I work / He works | for a small company.

I don't / He doesn't | work.

☐ **Possessives**

possessive adjectives

my, your, his, her, its, our, their
My sister's name is Ruth.

possessive forms of nouns

's: Carol's son is a writer. Carol's son's name is John.
s': Her daughters' names are Joanne and Betty.

USE ENGLISH TO

☐ **introduce someone formally**
Dr. Hummel, I'd like you to meet Jonathan Wilkins.

☐ **greet someone new**
It's nice to meet you.

☐ **greet someone I know informally**
Hi, John. How's it going?
OK, thanks, Nan.

☐ **leave a conversation politely**
Well, I'd better get back to work.

☐ **say goodbye formally**
Goodbye for now, Dr. Hummel.

☐ **say goodbye informally**
See you later, Jon.

☐ **talk about these subjects**
family members jobs names
where someone lives

☐ UNDERSTAND THESE EXPRESSIONS

He'd like to interview you.
(He) changes (his) mind (every day).
(He's) a good kid.
I'd better get back to (work).
(I'm) an only child.
(I'm) in charge of (the research department).
See you later.
What exactly (do you do there)?
Welcome to (MHI).

a family tree

CHECKLIST

Listening

1

A man is showing a friend pictures of his family.
Fill in each person's relation to the man. Use the words from the box.

grandfather	brother-in-law	grandmother	niece	father	nephew	mother	son
parents	daughter	sister	uncle	brother	aunt	sister-in-law	cousin

1. ....
2. ....
3. ....
4. ....
5. ....
6. ....

2

Jeanne is asking Marie about Marie's family. Mark the statements *T* (true) or *F* (false).

__ 1. Marie's husband's name is Mark.

__ 2. Marie and Mark have two children.

__ 3. One of their sons, Terry, is a dancer.

__ 4. Marie's sister lives in an apartment.

__ 5. Mark and Marie's son Bob is a student.

__ 6. Bob doesn't live on campus.

__ 7. Marie has two brothers.

__ 8. Jeanne and her husband have three children.

3

Marina Polis is the fifth international visitor to MHI. Listen to this interview and answer the questions about her. Circle the letter of the correct answer.

1. Where does she work?
   a. at a hospital
   b. at a school
2. What does she do there?
   a. She's a nurse.
   b. She's in charge of supplies.
3. Does she live and work in Athens?
   a. yes
   b. no
4. Does she live in a house or an apartment?
   a. a house
   b. an apartment
5. How many children does she have?
   a. three
   b. one
6. Where's her daughter?
   a. at the University of Michigan
   b. at Miami University

4

Give true answers.

1. ....
2. ....
3. ....
4. ....
5. ....
6. ....
7. ....
8. ....

Episode Three

People are walking on the deck of the *Princess* before dinner. Robert and Lucy are talking, looking at the sea and the evening sky.

Lucy says, "It's wonderful!"

Robert asks, "Is this your first trip to the Mediterranean?"

"It's my first cruise. And you?"

"No. I travel a lot for business."

"Oh, that's interesting."

The dining room is full. Agatha Jordan enters and finds Table 5. There are three people at the table: two men and a woman.

"Oh dear. Am I late? Please don't get up. I'm Agatha Jordan, Christina's aunt. She isn't coming to dinner. She's a little seasick."

"That's too bad," says one of the men, "I hope she feels better soon." He gives Agatha a big smile. "But I'm very happy to meet you, Mrs. Jordan. I'm Robert Grant."

"And I'm glad to meet you, Mr. Roberts."

"It's Grant, Mrs. Jordan, Robert Grant."

"I'm sorry, Mr. Grant. I'm very forgetful."

Robert Grant introduces the other people at the table. Lucy Cardozo is about 32. She's wearing black slacks and a silk blouse. Frank Adams is in his early 40s. He smiles a lot, but his eyes are sad.

"What do you do, Robert?" asks Frank.

"Real estate. We find houses in Spain and France, usually for Americans who want vacation homes in Europe."

Agatha turns to Lucy, "What do you do, Lucy?"

"I'm a fashion buyer. I'm in Europe to buy for the fall collections. The clothes in Paris this year have some beautiful colors."

"Really," says Agatha. "Who's your favorite designer?"

"My favorite is the Pierre Maurice collection. Pierre makes the most beautiful evening dresses," says Lucy.

"Oh yes. They're wonderful."

Robert sees the waiter coming to their table. "Oh, and speaking of wonderful, here comes dinner!"

Frank smiles, "Well, here we are. Our first evening. Four strangers on a boat with a week together in front of us."

Robert says, "A good idea for one of your stories, Frank, eh?"

"Are you a writer?"

"Yes, mysteries mainly. *The Hour of the Wolf, In the Evening Hours.* Do you know them?"

"Sorry, I don't," says Agatha.

"I don't read many mysteries," says Lucy.

Frank says, "Oh well!" He lifts his wine glass. "To an enjoyable and interesting cruise!"

Comprehension Check

1. What does Robert Grant do? Why does he travel a lot for his business?
2. What does Lucy Cardozo do? Why is she in Europe?
3. What do Agatha and Lucy talk about?
4. What does Frank Adams do?
5. Why doesn't Christina come to dinner?

UNIT 4

Secretary: Good morning, Dr. Lee's office.
Mr. Wolfe: Hello, this is Peter Wolfe. I'd like to make an appointment for a checkup.
Secretary: Can you come in on Monday, the 25th, at 9 AM?
Mr. Wolfe: Well, I work from 9 to 5 every day, but yes, I can.
Secretary: Good. What's your number at work, Mr. Wolfe?
Mr. Wolfe: 257-1310, extension 149.
Secretary: Thank you. We'll see you on the 25th then.

Doctor: Are you having any problems, Mr. Wolfe?
Mr. Wolfe: No, I feel great. I sleep well, eat right, get regular exercise.
Doctor: How often do you exercise?
Mr. Wolfe: Every day.

(later) . . .
Doctor: You're in very good shape, Mr. Wolfe.

Mr. Fox: Hello?
Secretary: Hello, Mr. Fox? This is Dr. Lee's office. We'd like to make an appointment for your annual checkup.
Mr. Fox: Oh, yeah, I got your card.
Secretary: Can you come in on Tuesday the 21st at 10:30?
Mr. Fox: No, I can't. I sleep late in the morning. Is the doctor ever there in the evening?
Secretary: Dr. Lee has evening hours on Thursdays. Can you make it on the 23rd at 7 o'clock?
Mr. Fox: Yeah, OK. That's Tuesday, the 23rd?
Secretary: No, Thursday, the 23rd. We'll see you then.

Doctor: Do you ever exercise, Mr. Fox? Go swimming? Jogging?
Mr. Fox: I can't swim, and I hate jogging.

(later) . . .
Doctor: Well, Mr. Fox, you have bad habits, but you're in good shape for a 50-year-old man.
Mr. Fox: But, Doctor, I'm only 26.
Doctor: I know.

Speaking

1

Add the words in parentheses ( ), and practice saying these questions and answers. They're from conversations with Mr. Wolfe and Mr. Fox. Use the chart below to help you.

When do you go to bed? *(usually)*
a. Oh, I go to bed at 2:00 or 3:00 AM. *(usually)*
b. I'm in bed at 11 o'clock. *(every night)*

When do you usually go to bed?
a. Oh, I usually go to bed at 2:00 or 3:00 AM.
b. I'm in bed at 11 o'clock every night.

1. How much sleep do you get? When do you get up? (usually)
   a. I get eight hours of sleep. (always)
      I get up at 7:00. (usually)
   b. It depends. I'm up at noon. (sometimes)
      I sleep until 3:00 or 3:30. (sometimes)

2. Do you eat a good breakfast? What do you have? (usually)
   a. I have juice, eggs, toast, cereal and coffee. (every day)
   b. I eat breakfast. (never)

3. What do you do in the evening? Do you go out? (ever)
   a. I go out. (five or six times a week)
   b. I read or watch TV. (sometimes)
      I go out during the week. (never)
      On weekends I go out. (about twice a month)

4. Do you take a vacation? (every year)
   a. Yes, I go camping in Alaska for two weeks. (every year)
   b. A vacation from what? I work. (never)
      I'm on vacation. (always)

- **A,** you're Dr. Lee. Ask Mr. Wolfe the questions above. **B,** you're Mr. Wolfe. Choose the right answers.

- **A,** this time you're Mr. Fox. **B,** you're Dr. Lee.

2

- American phone numbers look like this: (223) 555-1310.
Say them like this: *area code two two three//five five five//one three//one oh.*

Work numbers often have extensions, for example: 679-7300 ext. 149.
Say them like this: *six seven nine//seven three//oh oh//extension one four nine.*

- Have conversations like these:

At home

A: What's your phone number?
B: ....
724-3045
(623) 856-9568
your number

At work

A: What's your number at work?
B: ....
(425) 926-7652
896-2211 ext. 1271
your number

100%	ALWAYS
	USUALLY
50%	SOMETIMES
0%	NEVER

I	'm	always / usually / never		at home.
			have dinner	

	Do you	ever	exercise?
When		usually	

Sometimes I	'm / exercise	at home.

He exercises		every		day/night.
	(about)	once / twice / three times	a	week. / month. / year.

3

- Practice saying these times and days of the week.

AM		PM	
7:30	seven-thirty	3:00	....
8:00	eight/eight o'clock	4:30	four-thirty
9:00	....	5:15	....
9:45	....	6:05	six oh five
12:00	(twelve) noon	10:20	....
		12:00	(twelve) midnight

weekdays	**the weekend**	
Monday	Saturday	M–F = Monday through Friday
Tuesday	Sunday	Sat, 9–12 = Saturday, from 9:00 to 12:00
Wednesday		
Thursday		
Friday		

- Practice this conversation:

B: Hello.
A: Hello. Is this Ellen's Flowers?
B: Yes, it is.
A: Could you tell me when you're open?
B: Monday through Saturday from 10:00 to 3:00.
A: You close at 3:00?
B: That's right.
A: Thank you.

A

1. "Call" these places to find out when they're open. Write down their hours.

   Robert's Hardware
   ....
   ....

   Ames Department Store
   ....
   ....

   Ellen's Flowers
   ....
   ....

2. Answer B's questions. Use the information below.

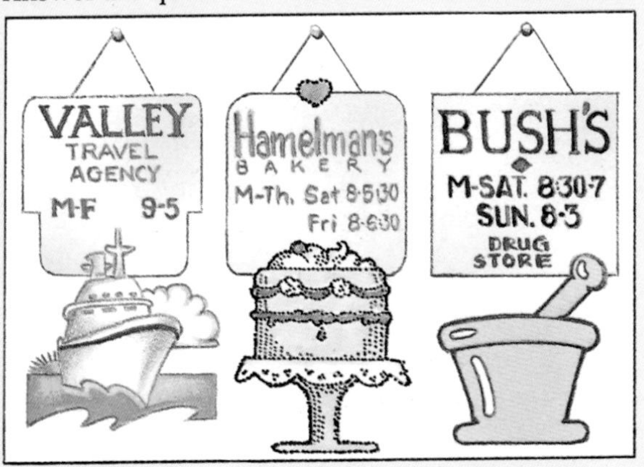

B

1. Answer A's questions. Use the information below.

2. "Call" these places to find out when they're open. Write down their hours.

   Valley Travel Agency
   ....
   ....

   Hamelman's Bakery
   ....
   ....

   Bush's Drugstore
   ....
   ....

4

Practice this conversation:

A: Dr. Gage's office.
B: Hello. This is Kathy Miller. I'd like to make an appointment for a checkup.
A: Can you come in on Monday at 3:00?
B: No, that day isn't good for me.
A: Can you make it on Tuesday at 10:00?
B: Yes, that's fine.
A: All right, we'll see you on Tuesday.

A

1. Call Dr. Gage's office and make an appointment at a time when you are free. You are not free at these times: Monday 4–6, Tuesday 12–2, Wednesday 10–12, Friday 12–1

2. Make an appointment for Dr. Gage. He can see people at these times:
Tuesday 10–11, Friday 2–3

B

1. Make an appointment for Dr. Gage. He can see people at these times:
Tuesday 1–2, Wednesday 10–11, Friday 9–10

2. Call Dr. Gage's office and make an appointment at a time when you are free. You are not free at these times: Monday 3–4:30, Tuesday 9–12, Wednesday 4–5, Friday 3–4:30

5

Pronunciation

Notice the differences between *can* and *can't* and practice saying these sentences.

I can týpe. I cȧn't týpe.

In questions and statements, *can* sounds like /**k'n**/.

Can you týpe? /**k'n**/ I can týpe. /**k'n**/

In short answers, *can* sounds like /**kan**/.

Yes, I cȧn. /**kan**/

Can't always sounds like /**kant**/.

I cȧn't týpe. /**kant**/ No, I cȧn't. /**kant**/

6

- Look at the words in this chart.

Can you . . . ?	A	B	C	D
dive/swim				
drive a car/motorcycle				
play the guitar/piano				
speak Chinese/Portuguese				
sing a song in English/in your language				
say the alphabet forwards (A-B-C . . .)/backwards (Z-Y-X . . .)				

- Find out what your partner can do, and fill in the chart.

A: Can you swim?
B: Yes, I can. OR No, I can't.

- **A** and **B,** join another pair (C and D) and tell each other about yourself and your partner. Then fill in the chart.

C: I can swim, and I can dive. D can swim, but she can't dive.
A: I can swim, but I can't dive. B can't swim, and he can't dive.

7

Culture Capsule

A typical big breakfast in the United States is bacon and eggs, toast with butter and jam, juice and coffee.

Do you usually eat breakfast?
What do you usually have for breakfast?

8

Elizabeth and Lannie Wright are twins. They look alike, but they have different jobs and different habits. They live at home with their mother, Mrs. Ruth Wright.

LANNIE: manages a restaurant

ELIZABETH: trains dogs

Ask and answer questions about Lannie and Elizabeth.
Use the information below.

A: Who works from 4:30 PM to 2:00 AM, Lannie or Elizabeth?
B: Lannie. Who goes jogging every morning?
A: Elizabeth. Who goes shopping in the afternoon?

Schedule

works from 4:30 PM to 2:00 AM
works from 8:00 AM to 3:00 or 4:00 PM
sleeps from 3:00 AM to 11:00 AM
sleeps from 10:00 PM to 5:30 AM

Activities

goes jogging every morning
goes shopping in the afternoon
visits friends during the day
goes to baseball games on weekends
reads in the evening
goes dancing on weekends
takes naps in the afternoon
stays home in the evening
takes a vacation in Hawaii
goes camping in Alaska

9

You want to know more about Lannie and Elizabeth. Ask their mother, Mrs. Wright.

- **A,** ask B (Mrs. Wright), about Lannie. **B,** you're Mrs. Wright. Answer A's questions.

A: When does Lannie usually get up?
B: At 11:00 AM.

1. When does she usually
   - get up?
   - get home?
   - go to work?
   - go to bed?
2. What does she usually do
   - during the day?
   - in the morning/afternoon/ evening?
   - on weekends?
3. Does she ever take a vacation?

- **B,** ask A (Mrs. Wright), about Elizabeth. **A,** you're Mrs. Wright. Answer B's questions.

10

Put It Together

A and **B,** ask each other about a typical weekday and a typical weekend day. Look at the questions in Exercise 9 for ideas. For example: *What time do you get up during the week? When do you usually get up on weekends? . . .*

I know how to . . .

CHECKLIST

USE THESE FORMS

☐ **Simple Present Tense**

The simple present tense describes habits or routines.

How much sleep do you get?
What does he do in the morning?
Do they ever go to the movies?
She goes shopping about once a month.

☐ **Frequency Expressions**

questions

Do you ever How often do you When do you usually	exercise?

statements

I	'm	always usually never		at home.
			have dinner	

Sometimes I	'm exercise	at home.

He exercises		every		day/night.
	(about)	once twice three times	a	week. month. year.

☐ **Time Expressions**

The doctor is here	at 9:00. from 9:00 to 5:30. until 5:00. Monday through Friday. on weekdays/weekends. in the morning/ afternoon/evening. during the day/week.

☐ **Can/Can't** *(expresses ability)*

I you he, she it we they	can/can't

questions

Can you swim?

short answers

Yes, I can.
No, I can't.

statements

I can swim.
I can't swim.

USE ENGLISH TO

☐ **ask for and give telephone numbers**
What's your number at work?
Area code (924) 257-1410, extension 149.

☐ **begin a telephone conversation**
Hello?
Hello, Mr. Fox? This is Dr. Lee's office.

☐ **make an appointment**
I'd like to make an appointment for a checkup.
Can you come in on Monday, the 25th, at 9:00 AM?
We'll see you then.

☐ **check that I understand something**
You close at 3:00?
That's right.

☐ **talk about ability**
I can swim, but I can't dive.

☐ **talk about these subjects**
telephone numbers   time
business hours   making appointments
abilities   habits   routines   breakfast   dates

☐ UNDERSTAND THESE EXPRESSIONS

Can you make it (on the 23rd)?
Good morning.
Goodbye.
It depends.
Yeah.

AM/PM
an annual checkup

be at home/at work
be up
be in (very) good shape
come in

get home
get up
get (8 hours of) sleep

go jogging/swimming/shopping/dancing
go to bed
go out

sleep late
stay home
take a vacation
take a nap

Listening

1

Write the phone numbers as you hear them.

1. .... 4. ....
2. .... 5. ....
3. .... 6. ....

2

Listen to the telephone conversations, and answer the questions.

1. What time does the Public Library open today? ....
2. When does the House of Pizza close tonight? ....
3. When does the Photo Factory open and close today? ....
4. Is the West Side Market open on Saturdays? ....
5. What time does the Steak Out Restaurant close tonight? .... Is it open on Sundays? .... On Tuesdays? ....

3

Do you hear *can* or *can't?* Circle the correct one.

1. Mary can/can't dance the samba. She can/can't dance the tango.
2. Joseph can/can't speak Portuguese. He can/can't speak Spanish.
3. Terry can/can't type. She can/can't take shorthand.
4. Bob can/can't meet his wife at 3:00. He can/can't meet her at 4:00.

4

Gus Tate plays on the Globals basketball team. Howard Shortell is asking him about his life.

Mark the statements *T* (true) or *F* (false).

Part 1: During the basketball season . . .

___ 1. Gus is never away from home.
___ 2. He usually eats in restaurants and sleeps in hotels.
___ 3. After a game, he goes back to the hotel and goes to bed.
___ 4. He never sleeps until 9:00 or 10:00.
___ 5. He never eats a big breakfast.
___ 6. He exercises every day.

Part 2: After the basketball season . . .

___ 7. Gus and his wife are usually at home.
___ 8. Gus never reads.
___ 9. Sometimes his wife watches TV.
___ 10. He usually gets up early.
___ 11. He goes to work every day.
___ 12. Gus never plays basketball.

5

Give true answers.

1. ....
2. ....
3. ....
4. ....
5. ....

MOON OF INDIA

Episode Four

After dinner, Frank, Lucy, Robert and Agatha are having coffee in the lounge. Robert invites them for a drink.

"No thanks, Robert," says Frank. I have to write tomorrow, and I need a good night's sleep."

Then Lucy says, "I'm feeling a little tired, too." She gets up to leave with Frank and asks Robert, "What about a swim tomorrow?"

"OK, but not too early." Robert turns to Agatha, "What about you? Will you have a drink with me?"

"That would be very nice but first I want to see how my niece is."

"Oh yes, Christina. I hope she's feeling better."

"I think she was just a little tired this evening."

"What can I get you to drink?"

"Mineral water, thank you Robert. I usually don't drink very much."

Robert is waiting on deck outside the lounge for Agatha. He is standing in a dark corner. Agatha returns and he watches her walking along the deck towards the lounge.

"Here's your drink."

Agatha is frightened. "Oh Robert!" She knocks the glass in Robert's hands. "Oh, I'm sorry."

"Don't worry about it. It doesn't matter. How's Christina?"

"She's much better, thank you."

"I'm glad to hear that. She's very nice."

"She's a special young woman: intelligent and hardworking, and . . . attractive, Robert. We're good friends. Once a year we take a trip together in Europe—Italy, Spain or Greece."

"Now tell me about yourself, Agatha."

"My life isn't very interesting. I'm a retired schoolteacher. I live in a little house in Vermont."

"And your husband?"

"Edgar died more than twenty years ago."

"I'm sorry to hear that. Do you have any children?"

"No. I don't."

"That's too bad."

"Is it, Robert? I have a beautiful niece. She's like a daughter to me. And thanks to Edgar, I have plenty of money in my retirement. You see, I'm very happy. I don't usually talk about myself so much, Robert. You're a good listener. But what about you? Tell me about yourself."

"Robert Grant, age 35, college educated, divorced, two children in Idaho. Present occupation: real estate agent for Estrellas Properties, Costa del Sol, Spain. That's me."

"There's more to you than that, Robert, I'm sure."

Robert looks at Agatha and smiles a big smile.

"Christina was right," she thinks. "He's a very handsome man."

Comprehension Check

1. Why don't Lucy and Frank want to stay for a drink after dinner?
2. Where does Agatha go before she has a drink with Frank?
3. Are Agatha and Christina like mother and daughter?
4. How does Agatha describe Christina?
5. What do you know about Agatha now?
6. What do you know about Robert now?

UNIT 5

1. Excuse me? What did you say? I didn't hear you. Oh, yes, I knew James Dean very well. His parents were Mildred and Winton Dean. Jimmy was born right here in Marion, Indiana. That was in, uh, 1931. Times weren't good then. There were no jobs, and his parents didn't have much money. They moved to California in '35. Then Jimmy's mother died, and he came back to Indiana. He grew up in Fairmount, on his uncle's farm.

2. Jimmy and I were in school together. We graduated from Fairmount High in 1949. He didn't like school very much, but he liked sports, and he was good at them. You know, he wasn't especially good-looking. He was short and thin, and he wore glasses. But he had something. Maybe I was a little in love with him then. Later, the whole world was.

3. I met James Dean here in Hollywood in '49. I was in the movie *Giant,* too, but you probably don't remember me. I was never a star like Jimmy. He was a wonderful actor. He died too young. It was a car accident, on September 30, 1955. That was a long time ago, but I still remember him. A lot of people do.

IN MEMORY OF JAMES

THE FAIRMOUNT NEW

Volume LXXX

Fairmount, Grant County, Indiana

James Dean Killed

Of California Car A

FAIRMOUNT IS STUNNED TO LEARN OF TRAGEDY WHICH CLAIMED NATIVE SON; HEADON COLLISION NEAR INTERSECTION CAUSES FATALITY FRIDAY

. . . a Student at U.C.L.A.

James Dean

Last Rites W

Held Here Sat

Basketball Star

DEATH OF JAMES DEAN, FAIRMOUNT HIGH ALUMNI CASTS A PALL OF SADNESS OVER STUDENT BODY

$105,000 ESTATE LEFT BY ACTOR JIMMY DEAN

Speaking

1

- First Interview:

Complete these questions with *was, were* or *did.* Then answer them.

1. Who .... James Dean's parents?
2. Where .... he born?
3. .... times good in 1931?
4. .... his parents have much money?
5. When .... they move to California?
6. .... James Dean grow up in Fairmount, Indiana?

- Second and Third Interviews:

A, ask B questions about the information in the second interview.
B, ask A questions about the information in the third interview.

2

- Ask your partner about his/her life.

A: Where .... you born?
B: In ....
A: .... you grow up there?
B: Yes, ...
OR No, ...
I .... in ....
A: Where .... you go to high school?
B: ....
OR I'm still in high school.
A: .... like school?
B: ....
A: .... sports?
B: ....
A: .... good at them?
B: ....

- **A** and **B,** join another pair of students. Tell them about your partner. Use the information from Exercise 2.

3
Movie Match

Which movies were these actors and actresses in? Ask questions with *was* and *were.*

A: Was/Were *(actor or actors)* in *(movie)* ?
B: Yes, ... was/were.
OR No, ... wasn't/weren't. Try again!

A

1. Ask B which movies these actors and actresses were in.

Actors and Actresses

Barbra Streisand
Meryl Streep and Robert Redford
Arnold Schwarzenegger
Humphrey Bogart and Katharine Hepburn
Harrison Ford

Movies

Out of Africa
The Terminator
Funny Girl
Raiders of the Lost Ark
The African Queen

2. Answer B's questions.

Back to the Future: Michael J. Fox
Butch Cassidy and the Sundance Kid: Paul Newman and Robert Redford
The Godfather: Marlon Brando
Superman: Marlon Brando and Christopher Reeve
Help!: The Beatles

B

1. Answer A's questions.

Raiders of the Lost Ark: Harrison Ford
Out of Africa: Meryl Streep and Robert Redford
The Terminator: Arnold Schwarzenegger
Funny Girl: Barbra Streisand
The African Queen: Humphrey Bogart and Katharine Hepburn

2. Ask A which movies these actors and actresses were in.

Actors

Marlon Brando
The Beatles
Paul Newman and Robert Redford
Marlon Brando and Christopher Reeve
Michael J. Fox

Movies

Butch Cassidy and the Sundance Kid
The Godfather
Superman
Help!
Back to the Future

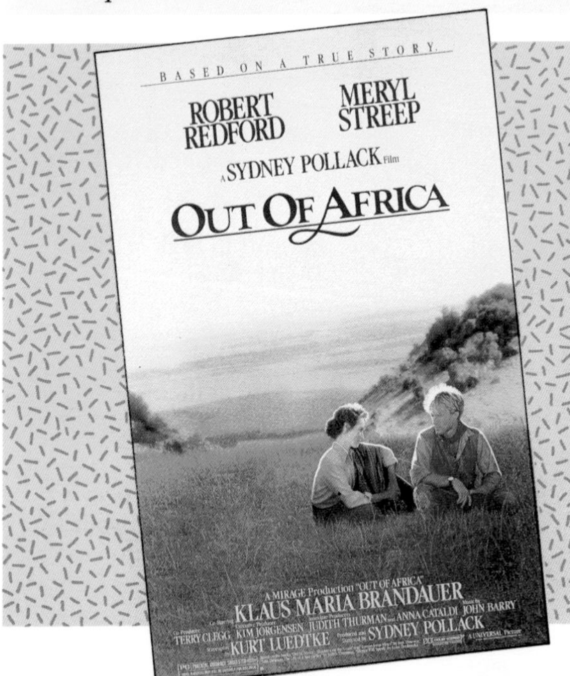

4

Ask and answer questions about these people.

1. Is Susan short?
2. Does Harry have black hair?
3. Does Tom wear glasses?
4. Does Mary have brown hair?
5. Does Harry wear glasses?
6. Is Harry thin?

5

- Describe these people. Use the words in Exercise 4.

I	-	me
you	-	....
she	-	her
he	-	....
we	-	....
they	-	....

- You went to high school with the people in the picture.

Practice this conversation:

A: You know, I saw Peggy Mills last week. Do you remember her?
B: I'm not sure. Was she short?
A: No, she was tall.
B: Did she have blond hair?
A: Yes, she did.
B: Did she wear glasses?
A: Yes.
B: Oh, I remember her.
A: Well, she's an actress now.
B: Really!

A

You saw Nancy Mack (c) and Ginny Call (f). Nancy's a doctor and Ginny's a writer now.

Conversation 1:
Tell B about Nancy.

Conversation 3:
Tell B about Ginny.

B

You saw Larry Slocum (b) and Ken Gant (e). Larry's a computer salesman and Ken's an English teacher now.

Conversation 2:
Tell A about Larry.

Conversation 4:
Tell A about Ken.

6
Pronunciation

Some verbs add a **t** or a **d** sound for past tense. Others add an **əd** sound for past tense.

/**t**/	/**d**/	/**əd**/
liked	moved	graduated
....	....	....
....	....	....

Do Exercise 7. Then add verbs to these lists.

7

Famous Dates

January	April	July	October
February	May	August	November
March	June	September	December

in | May
   | 1962

on | May 28
   | May 28, 1962

- Practice saying these dates:

5/28/02 May twenty-eighth nineteen oh two
6/1/83 June first nineteen eighty-three

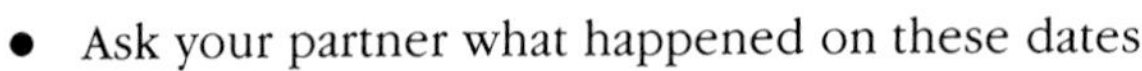

- Ask your partner what happened on these dates.

A: What happened on April 6, 1909?
B: (I think) Peary reached the North Pole.
OR I don't know.

4/6/09	JOHN F. KENNEDY DIES
1876	PEARY REACHES THE NORTH POLE
5/21/27	THE OLYMPICS OPEN IN SEOUL
11/22/63	BELL INVENTS THE TELEPHONE
7/20/69	MEN LAND ON THE MOON
9/88	LINDBERGH CROSSES THE ATLANTIC ALONE

- Now finish Exercise 6.

8

A, ask your partner what he or she did at these times:

(earlier) today

yesterday morning/afternoon/evening

last night/Tuesday/week/month

B, give true information. Use these words: *went (to), ate, studied, worked from . . . to, read, watched.*

A: What did you do yesterday morning?
B: I went to the store.

9
Put It Together

Draw a line like this. List the important events in your life. Put the dates on the line.

8/11/35 ———————— Today

A, tell B about events in your life. **B,** ask questions. Use the events and questions below for ideas.

EVENTS

- was born on...
- went to school in...
- graduated from...
- started working in...
- got married...
- moved to...

QUESTIONS

- Where were you born?
- Where's that?
- How many people were there in your class?
- Do you still work there?
- What's your husband's/wife's name? How did you meet him/her?
- Do you still live there?

I know how to . . .

USE THESE FORMS

☐ **Simple Past Tense of Be**

I he, she it	was wasn't	you we they	were weren't

questions
Was Barbra Streisand in "Funny Girl"?
Where were you born?

short answers
Yes, she was.
No, she wasn't.

statements
Jimmy was born in Marion, Indiana.
He wasn't especially good-looking.

☐ **Simple Past Tense of Other Verbs**

I you he, she we they	graduated didn't graduate

questions
What happened on April 6, 1909?
What did you say?
Did you grow up there?

short answers
Yes, I did.
No, I didn't.

statements
I met James Dean in '49.
James wore glasses then, but he didn't wear them in his movies.

Irregular verbs (see page 119)

Regular verbs

/**t**/	/**d**/	/**əd**/
liked	remembered	graduated

☐ **Past Time Expressions**

yesterday earlier this	morning afternoon evening	last	night Tuesday week month	in	November 1968	on	November 14 November 14, 1968

☐ **Object Pronouns**
me, you, him, her, it, us, them — He remembers me.

USE ENGLISH TO

☐ **ask someone to repeat something**
Excuse me? What did you say?

☐ **hesitate**
Uh . . .

☐ **describe someone**
He was short and thin, and he wore glasses.

☐ **talk about these subjects**
recent past events — important events in people's lives — famous people

☐ UNDERSTAND THESE EXPRESSIONS

Times weren't good then.
We were in school together.

be born
be good at
be good-looking

be in love with
come back to
grow up

graduate from

CHECKLIST

Listening

1

You'll hear eight questions. Some are in the present tense. Some are in the past tense. Check (✓) the correct column.

	Present	Past
1.	☐	☐
2.	☐	☐
3.	☐	☐
4.	☐	☐
5.	☐	☐
6.	☐	☐
7.	☐	☐
8.	☐	☐

2

Complete the conversations. Choose *a* or *b*.

1. a. Yes, he was.
   b. Yes, they were.
2. a. No, he wasn't.
   b. No, he didn't.
3. a. I don't remember her.
   b. I don't remember him.
4. a. I don't know.
   b. Yes, he did.
5. a. In August.
   b. On the 11th.
6. a. He directed movies.
   b. Yes, he was.

3

Match the celebrity with his or her date of birth.

___	1. Clint Eastwood	a. 7/26/43
___	2. Mick Jagger	b. 9/16/25
___	3. Jane Fonda	c. 1/28/48
___	4. B. B. King	d. 5/31/30
___	5. Woody Allen	e. 8/9/64
___	6. Whitney Houston	f. 12/1/35
___	7. Mikhail Baryshnikov	g. 12/21/37

4

Give true answers.

1. ....
2. ....
3. ....
4. ....
5. ....
6. ....

Episode Five

Back in New York at the police station. The police captain enters Lieutenant Washington's office. Washington is speaking to a newspaper reporter on the telephone. "The investigation is making progress. . . . I can't answer that question. Yes, we're working with Interpol. . . . Yes. . . . No. . . . Yes. . . . Goodbye." Turning to the Captain, "That was the tenth telephone call today."

"Progress on the investigation, I hear."

"Some. . . . We know that Richardson's killer and the Moon of India are on the ship. We think the killer wants to sell it when the *Princess* arrives in Marseilles."

"Who is the killer?"

"We think we know but we're not sure yet."

"We'd better find out soon. The museum wants the necklace back and I want to find the killer."

"We're doing our best, sir. We have one of our best officers on the ship."

Thousands of miles away on the ship, the sun is shining. Agatha, Christina, Frank and Robert are sitting around the swimming pool. Christina is reading a newspaper.

"This is very interesting," she says.

"What is, dear?" asks Agatha.

"The Moon of India is still missing from the City Museum."

"Christina works in the City Museum, Frank."

"Yes," replies Frank, "Christina told me yesterday that her specialty is Egyptian art."

"Do you know the Moon of India, Christina?" asks Robert.

"Yes, but it wasn't in my department, so I didn't see it often. Listen to this." She reads from the paper: "'The famous necklace disappeared from the City Museum the night of April 16. Museum employees discovered the loss early the next morning.' The police, it says, are working day and night."

"What does it say about the necklace?" asks Robert.

"Let's see." Christina reads from the paper again: "'The Moon of India has 45 perfect diamonds. It was a wedding present for the Princess of Aipur in 1771.'"

"Wow!" says Frank.

"The necklace is worth more than four million dollars."

"Four million dollars. That's a lot of money," says Frank.

"Yes," says Robert, "an incredible amount of money."

Lucy arrives in a swimsuit. "Let's go swimming!" She dives into the pool, followed by Robert.

Comprehension Check

1. Where is the necklace? Does Richardson's killer have it?
2. Who is the killer? Do the police know?
3. What do the police think the killer wants to do with the necklace?
4. Is there a police detective on the ship?
5. What do you know about the Moon of India?
6. Does Christina know the Moon of India?

UNIT 6

Harry: Tom! How are you?
Tom: Harry, you look great! How's it going?
Harry: Not bad. It's good to see you. How's your family?
Tom: They're fine.
Harry: How are the kids?
Tom: Well, my boy Danny is taking a course in computers.
Harry: Is he still working at the grocery store?
Tom: Yes, but he wants to change jobs. He has a family now, and he needs to make more money. How about your children? What's Michael doing these days? Is he still living in California?
Harry: Not anymore. He moved to Oregon, and now he's raising sheep.
Tom: Raising sheep? How does he like it?
Harry: Well, it's hard work, but he really likes it.
Tom: And your daughter? She works in New York, right?
Harry: Paula usually works in New York, but she's working on a special project in D.C. this year.

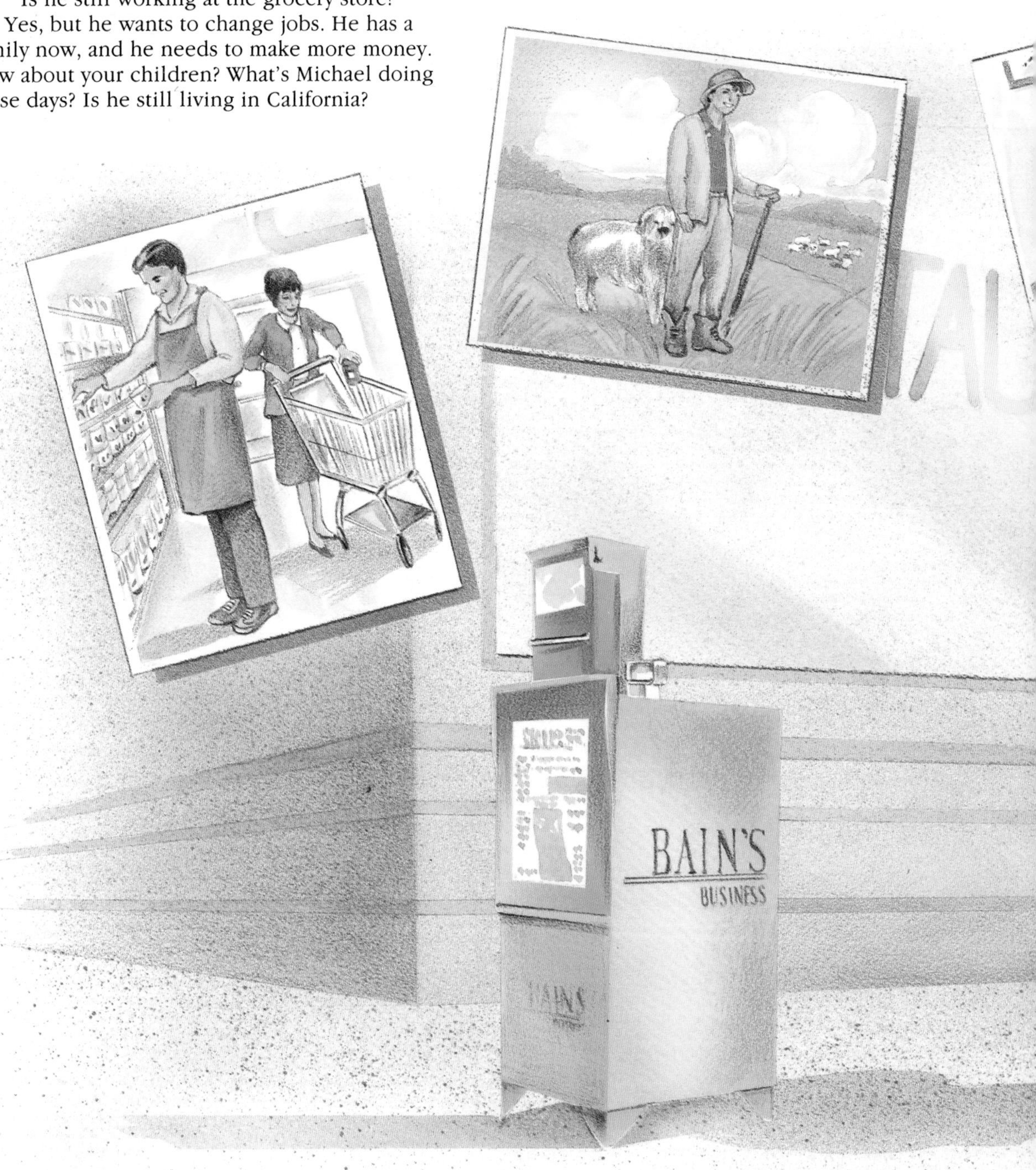

Tom: And your wife?
Harry: Well, she's fine. She went back to college, you know, and now . . . I'd better go! She's probably waiting for me right now.
Tom: OK. It was really good seeing you.
Harry: Same here. Take it easy.

Speaking

1

Look at the pictures. Ask and answer questions about what people are doing.

Danny

A: What's Danny doing?
B: Putting cans on the shelf.

1. Danny
2. the customer
3. Michael
4. Paula
5. Harry's wife

---

wait for Harry, look at her watch
write a report
shop
put cans on the shelf
take a walk

2

Look at the pictures. Ask and answer questions about what people are wearing.

Tom

A: What's Tom wearing?
B: A brown jacket and tan pants.

1. Tom
2. Harry's wife
3. Paula
4. Michael
5. Danny
6. the customer
7. Harry

---

skirt
blouse
sweater
dress
pants
jeans
shirt
apron
suit
tie
jacket
high-heeled shoes
sneakers
boots
hat

3

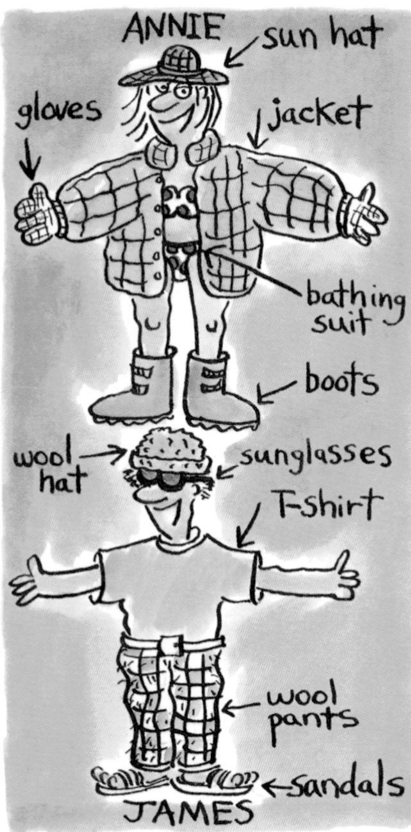

A, study the picture of Annie. **B**, study the picture of James. **A**, close your book. **B**, ask A "What's Annie wearing?" **B**, close your book. **A**, ask B "What's James wearing?"

4

A, you're packing for a trip to Alaska. **B**, you're packing for a trip to Hawaii.

- Look at James' and Annie's clothes. Ask and answer questions like these:

A: Do you need a sun hat?
B: Yes, I do.
A: Do you need a jacket?
B: No, I don't.

- Summarize your lists: I need to take . . . .

5

Culture Capsule

In general, Americans like to dress casually. They don't like to wear very formal clothes. In some other countries, people dress formally.

What do teachers in your country usually wear in the classroom?
What do people usually wear in a restaurant?
What do people usually wear in a supermarket?
What do you usually wear in a restaurant? In a supermarket?

6

Do You Remember?

- Describe your partner's clothes. Begin: You're wearing . . .

- **A**, does B remember what you're wearing? Ask questions. **B**, don't look at A. Answer his or her questions.

A: Am I wearing black shoes?
B: Yes, you are. OR No, you're not. You're wearing brown shoes.
A: You're right. OR Try again!

7

	Title of Course	Days	Times	Room	Instructor
English					
101-01	English Composition	MWF	10:00-10:55am	265	Henderson
102-01	Intro to Literature	MWF	11:00-11:55am	265	Michaels
Science					
205-02	Biology	MWF	10:00-10:55am	161	Jones
201-01	Principles of Chemistry	MWF	1:00-1:55pm	160	Gates
Social Sciences					
221	Child Psychology	MWF	2:30-3:30pm	270	Sage
101-01	Intro to Anthropology	MW	3:00-4:20pm	156	Fantini
201-01	Principles of Economics	MWF	10:00-10:55am	151	Moran
201-02	Principles of Economics	T Th	5:00-6:20pm	151	Moran
History					
901-03	European History	T Th	1:00-1:20pm	220	Stern
869-01	History of Mexico	MWF	11:00-11:55am	266	Silverman

Intro = introduction

- **A** and **B**, you're registering for your classes. You each need one more course in your schedule. Look at the course list above, and add one more course to your schedule.

	MON	TUES	WED	THURS	FRI
AM					
PM	1-1:55 CHEMISTRY RM 160 Prof GATES 2:30-3:30 CHILD PSYCHOLOGY RM 270 SAGE		1-1:55 CHEM 2:30-3:30 CHILD PSYCH		1-1:55 CHEM 2:30-3:30 CHILD PSYCH

A's schedule

- It's a month later. Have conversations like this:

A: What courses are you taking?
B: I'm taking European History, Biology and ....
A: How do you like your history course?
B: A lot. OR It's OK. OR Not very much.
A: Who's teaching it?
B: ....
A: How do you like ....?
B: ....

	MON	TUES	WED	THURS	FRI
AM	10-10:55 BIOLOGY RM 161 PROF JONES		10-10:55 BIOLOGY		10-10:55 BIO
PM		1-2:20 EUROPEAN HISTORY PROF STERN RM 220		1-1:20 HISTORY	

B's schedule

8

A and **B**, you are classmates. **A**, ask B about the biology and history classes. **B**, ask A about the chemistry and psychology classes. Use the information from the course list on page 44 and the schedule changes below to answer.

SCHEDULE CHANGES THIS WEEK

201-01	Principles of Chemistry	T Th	10:00-11:20	Hawkinson
221-01	Child Psychology	M F	5:00-6:20	Freeman
205-02	Biology	M F	5:00-6:20	Stanley
901-03	European History	M W	3:00-4:20	Millett

biology

A: You know, I'd like to go to your biology class some time. When does it meet?
B: Well, it usually meets on Mondays, Wednesdays and Fridays from 10:00 to 10:55, but this week it's meeting on Monday and Friday from 5:00 to 6:20 in the evening.
A: Where does it meet?
B: Room 161.
A: Who's teaching it?
B: Well, Professor Jones usually teaches it, but this week Professor Stanley is teaching it.
A: Hmm, maybe this isn't a good week to go.

9

- Have conversations like this:

A: What's Mary doing these days? Is she still studying Spanish?
B: Not anymore. Now she's studying Japanese.
A: Studying Japanese?
B: Yes, she wants to travel to Japan.

A, ask questions as in the example.

Mary	live in New York
Peter	study Spanish
John	work as a waiter
Kate	work at the grocery store

B, use this information to answer A's questions.

look for another job	make more money
study Japanese	learn Spanish
live in Mexico	be an accountant
study accounting	travel to Japan

- **A** and **B**, ask each other these questions. Give true answers.

Are you taking any courses? What courses are you taking? When do they meet? How do you like them?

Do you work? What hours do you work? What do you usually do at work? Are you working on any special projects?

10
Pronunciation

Practice this conversation. Ask the questions with real interest.

A: ......*(Name)*......! How are you?
B: I'm fine, thanks, ...*(Name)*...... How're you?
A: OK. How's your family?
B: Everybody's fine. Yours?
A: Great. How're the kids?
B: Well, my son has a new job.
A: How does he like it?

11
Put It Together

A and **B**, on a separate piece of paper, write down the information about your life three years ago. Give your partner the piece of paper.

Look at the information about your partner. You haven't seen your partner in three years. You meet again. Find out about your partner.

A: ......*(Name)*......! It's good to see you! How are you?
B: I'm fine, thanks ......*(Name)*...... How are you? Are you still living in ....?
A: ....

3 Years Ago

Residence:

Job:

Activities:

Information about family:

I know how to . . .

CHECKLIST

USE THESE FORMS

☐ **Present Continuous Tense**

I	am ('m) 'm not	working

he she it	is ('s) isn't	working

you we they	are ('re) aren't	working

questions
What's she wearing?
Are you working at the bank?

short answers
Yes, I am. No, I'm not.

statements
She's wearing a brown leather jacket.
Danny is taking a course in computers.

The present continuous is used for action happening right now.
What's she wearing?

It is also used for action over an "extended" present time.
What are you doing these days?

Some verbs don't usually take the continuous: be, have, like, need, want.
He likes to speak Japanese.
NOT ~~He's liking~~ to speak Japanese.

The present continuous contrasts with the simple present.
He usually works in D.C., but this year he's working in Boston.

☐ **Still/Anymore**

question
Is he still living in California?

statements
He's still working at the grocery store.
(He's) not (living in California) anymore.

USE ENGLISH TO

☐ **greet someone informally**
Tom! How are you?
Harry, you look great! How's it going?
Not bad. It's good to see you.

☐ **ask about someone's family**
How's your family? How are the kids?/And your husband?
They're/He's fine.

☐ **ask about someone's activities**
What's Michael doing these days?
He's raising sheep.
Raising sheep? How does he like it?

☐ **say goodbye informally**
It was really good seeing you.
Same here. Take it easy.

☐ **talk about these subjects**
clothes college courses work activities

☐ UNDERSTAND THESE EXPRESSIONS

How does (he) like (it)?
It's good to see you.
It's hard work.

change jobs
go back to college
make money
pack for a trip
take a course in . . .
work on a special project

Listening

1

Alice is a stranger. She doesn't know the people at the party. Dennis knows some of the people at the party. Listen to this conversation between Alice and Dennis. Match the people in the picture with the names below.

1. Monica ___ 2. Joe ___ 3. Joan ___ 4. Melanie ___
5. Mark ___ 6. Fred ___ 7. Sue ___ 8. Jessica ___

2

Complete the conversations. Choose *a* or *b*.

1. a. Not anymore.
   b. He really likes it.
2. a. Because she wants to change jobs.
   b. She's probably studying.
3. a. Yes, she does.
   b. Very much.
4. a. Yes, I am.
   b. Yes, I do.
5. a. No, he isn't.
   b. Yes, he does.
6. a. On Tuesdays and Fridays.
   b. Not very much.
7. a. She usually eats lunch at 12:00.
   b. She's probably eating lunch.
8. a. Yes, I do.
   b. No, I don't.

3

Give true answers.

1. ....
2. ....
3. ....
4. ....

Episode Six

It is the next evening. Agatha and Christina are getting ready for dinner. Christina is looking in the mirror, trying to decide which necklace to wear. There is a knock at the door. It's Frank.

"Are you ladies ready for dinner?"

"Come in, Frank. We'll be ready in a minute."

"Take your time, the night is young."

"You're happy tonight, Frank," says Christina.

"Yes, I did some good work on my book this afternoon."

"Really? Tell us about it."

"Well, you know, that Moon of India story gave me the idea. I'm going to write a story about a famous necklace that is stolen from a museum. The thief takes the necklace on a ship and plans to sell it at one of the ship's ports, but can't because . . . guess why!"

"The police know what's happening," Christina guesses.

"Right. There's a detective on the ship."

Christina asks him, "What happens next?"

Frank walks over to a painting on the cabin wall. "I don't know yet. A good mystery is like a painting. Large parts of it are very dark. But when we look at the painting a second, a third, a fourth time, we see more. When you read a detective story, you need to look into the dark; slowly you begin to see the story."

The dining room is full of people. People are talking and laughing. Waiters are pouring water and bringing large menus to every table. At table five, Frank remembers that he left his glasses in the Jordans' cabin.

"I'll go back and get them for you," offers Christina.

"No, please, you stay here," says Frank, "I'll go and get them."

"OK, here's the key to the room."

Frank walks quickly to the Jordans' cabin, unlocks the door, goes in and gets his glasses. In a hurry to get back to the dining room, he forgets to close the door when he goes out. A few minutes later, Robert Grant comes to the door of the Jordans' cabin. The door is open and he goes inside. A purser watches him go in.

"Christina? Agatha? Anybody home? Hello?"

The purser hears him and enters the room.

"Can I help you, Sir?"

"The door was open," Robert begins to explain. "I thought they were here."

"I think they're in the dining room, sir."

"Thank you."

"Good evening, sir."

They leave the cabin.

Comprehension Check

1. Why is Frank happy?
2. What is his idea for a story?
3. Why is reading a good mystery like looking at a painting?
4. What did Frank leave in the Jordans' cabin?
5. Who goes into the cabin after Frank?

UNIT 7

Joan: How about some peaches? Do we have any at home?
David: Not many. Why don't we get some?
Joan: How much are the peaches?
Salesman: Fifty-nine cents a pound. They're on sale this week. How many would you like?
Joan: That's a good price! I'd like two pounds, please.
Salesman: Would you like anything else?
Joan: That's all, thank you.

Richard: The bread looks great. Should we get some?
Sue: It depends. How much is it?
Richard: Only a dollar a loaf.
Sue: That's not bad. Let's get a loaf.
Richard: How about some cookies? They look delicious.
Sue: They're kind of expensive, and we still have a lot of cookies at home. I don't think we need any.

Saleswoman 1: Can I help you?
Kim: No, thanks. We're just looking.

Saleswoman 2: Pam, I need some change. Do you have any?
Saleswoman 1: Yes, some. How much do you need?
Saleswoman 2: Not much, just some quarters.

Speaking

1

Ask and answer questions about American money.

A: How many pennies are there in a dollar?
B: A hundred. How many nickels are there in a quarter?

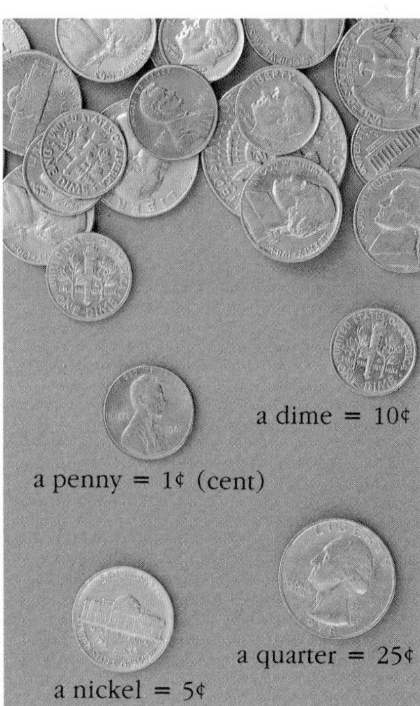

2

Use the money you have with you right now in class and practice this conversation:

A: I need some change. Do you have any?
B: Yes, some/a lot/but not much. How much do you need?
A: Not much. Just some ....

OR

A: I need some change. Do you have any?
B: No, I don't. Sorry.
A: That's OK.

3

Practice saying these prices. Then **A**, ask B: *How much is/are the . . . ?*
B, answer with the information below.

A

1. Have four conversations like this:

A: The .... look/s good. Should we get some?
B: It depends. How much is it/are they?
A: ....
B: That's not bad. Let's get some.
OR That's kind of expensive.
I don't think we need any.

lemon cookies	45¢/each
rye bread	$2/loaf

Conversation 1:
You want the rye bread.

Conversation 3:
You want the lemon cookies.

2. Have four conversations like this:

A: Do we have any ....?
B: Not much./Not many.
A: Let's get some.
OR Why don't we get some?
B: How much is it/are they?
A: ....
B: That's a good price. How many/much should we get?
A: ....

cherries	$2/lb.
jam	$3/jar

Conversation 1:
You want the jam.

Conversation 3:
You want the cherries.

B

1. Have four conversations like this:

A: The .... look/s good. Should we get some?
B: It depends. How much is it/are they?
A: ....
B: That's not bad. Let's get some.
OR That's kind of expensive.
I don't think we need any.

apple pie	95¢/piece
whole wheat rolls	$3/doz.

Conversation 2:
You want the whole wheat rolls.

Conversation 4:
You want the apple pie.

2. Have four conversations like this:

A: Do we have any ....?
B: Not much./Not many.
A: Let's get some.
OR Why don't we get some?
B: How much is it/are they?
A: ....
B: That's a good price. How many/much should we get?
A: ....

bananas	49¢/lb.
honey	$2/jar

Conversation 2:
You want the bananas.

Conversation 4:
You want the honey.

4

Pronunciation

- Listen for the difference in these numbers:

13	thirteen	30	thirty
14	fourteen	40	forty
15	fifteen	50	fifty
16	sixteen	60	sixty
17	seventeen	70	seventy
18	eighteen	80	eighty
19	nineteen	90	ninety

- Practice these numbers in conversations like this:

A: How much are these?
B: Fifteen cents/dollars each.
A: Excuse me? Did you say fifteen or fifty?
B: Fifteen.

There are different ways to say prices in English. For example,

$1.50 can be:
a dollar and fifty cents OR
one fifty. (This is how we usually say it.)

$2.05 can be:
two dollars and five cents OR
two oh five.

Practice saying these amounts:

$1.75	$3.09	$24.95
$1.99	$2.19	....
$7.05	$19.39	....

6

Go Shopping!

Take turns as shopper and shopkeeper. Shopkeeper: Decide prices. Shopper: You have $5.00. Practice conversations like this:

A: Can I help you?
B: Yes, please. How much is/are the ....?
A: .... a pound. How many/much would you like?
B: .... pound(s), please.
A: Would you like anything else?
B: Yes, I'd like. . . . OR No, that's all. Thank you.

7

- Do you know the names for these containers?

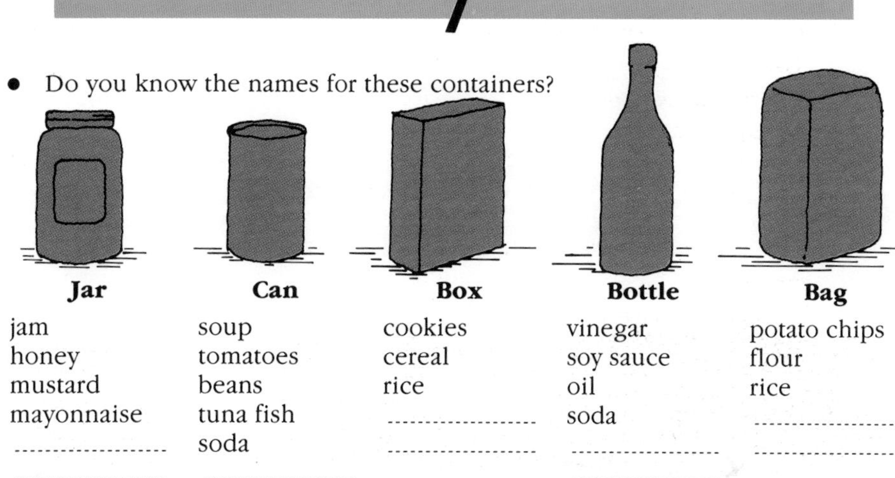

Jar	**Can**	**Box**	**Bottle**	**Bag**
jam	soup	cookies	vinegar	potato chips
honey	tomatoes	cereal	soy sauce	flour
mustard	beans	rice	oil	rice
mayonnaise	tuna fish	....	soda	....
....	soda	....	....	....
....	....		....	

- Practice saying *a jar of jam, a can of soup. . . .*

8

A's LIST
jam
soup
cereal
vinegar
oil
rice
flour
juice
B's LIST
mustard
beans
soda
rice
cookies
soy sauce
potato chips
oil

- The food on your list is on the check-out counter. Match your list and the containers on the counter.

- You arrive home from the grocery store. Your partner asks:

A: What did you buy?
B: I bought two jars of mustard, a bottle of oil, etc.

9
Culture Capsule

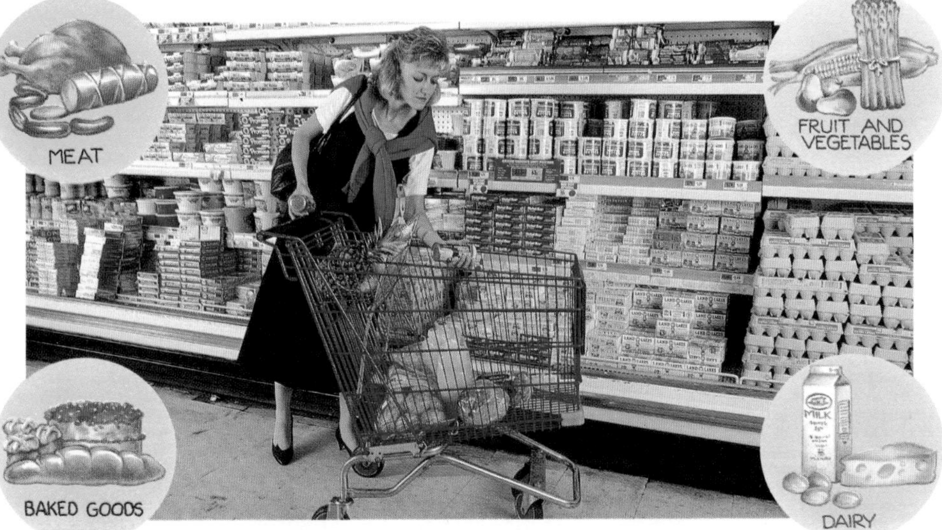

Most Americans shop in supermarkets because they can buy meat, vegetables, fruit, dairy products and baked goods in one store. They don't usually go shopping every day, but they buy a lot of food on one shopping trip.

Where do people in your country usually shop for food? Do they buy meat at the butcher or in a supermarket? Do they buy fruit and vegetables in a small market or in a supermarket? Do they buy baked goods at a bakery?

Where do you shop for food? How often do you go grocery shopping? When was the last time you went food shopping? What did you buy?

10
Put It Together

Hamburgers and apple pie are favorite dishes in the United States. What are some favorite dishes in your country?

A, choose a favorite dish from your country. What do you need in order to make this dish? Make a shopping list. For example: *For apple pie you need flour, butter, apples, cinnamon and sugar.*

B, help A to make a shopping list. Ask A "What do you need?" and "How much/many do you need?" Use the chart below to help you.

B, choose some of the items from A's shopping list. Write prices next to them. You are the shopkeeper.

A, go to B's store, and ask for the items on your list.

Countable
How many .....?

a pound of	apples bananas carrots oranges peaches string beans tomatoes
a dozen	eggs cookies rolls

Uncountable
How much .....?

a pound of	butter cheese coffee honey flour sugar

I know how to . . .

CHECKLIST

USE THESE FORMS

☐ **Countable and Uncountable Nouns and Quantifiers**

COUNTABLE

singular		*plural*	
one a	peach	two some a pound of a lot of not many not any	peaches

questions
Do we have any (peaches)?
How many (peaches) do we need?

statements
We don't have many (peaches).
We have a lot.
We don't need any.

UNCOUNTABLE

some a pound of not much a lot of not any	bread

questions
Do we have any (bread)?
How much (bread) do we need?

statements
We don't have much (bread).
We have a lot.
We don't need any.

USE ENGLISH TO

☐ **make suggestions**
Let's get a loaf.
How about some cookies?
Why don't we get some?

☐ **ask someone's opinion**
Should we get some?

☐ **talk to a customer**
Can I help you?
How many peaches would you like?
Would you like anything else?

☐ **talk to a salesperson**
How much is it?
Three dollars a pound.
I'd like two pounds, please.
That's all, thank you.

☐ **talk about these subjects**
food shopping money prices containers

☐ UNDERSTAND THESE EXPRESSIONS

It depends.
(The bread) looks great/delicious.
(They're) kind of expensive.
(They're) on sale this week.
We're/I'm just looking.

Listening

1

Maggie and John are making a shopping list.
Listen to their conversation, and complete the list.

2

Fill in the missing prices.

THIS WEEK'S SPECIALS
☆ ☆ ☆ ☆ ☆
FIRST NATIONAL SUPERMARKET
string beans ____ lb
tomato soup 59 ¢ / can
Soup
Red Delicious apples ____ / lb
rye bread 99 ¢ / loaf
eggs ____ / dozen
butter ___ / lb
dinner rolls $ 1.80 / dozen
American cheese ___ / lb
bananas 45 ¢ / lb
strawberry jam ___ / 1 lb jar

3

What did Mr. Harriman buy?

10 .... of ....

3 .... of ....

7 .... of ....

6 .... of ....

8 .... of ....

5 .... of ....

4 .... of ....

3 dozen ....

4

Give true answers.

1. ....
2. ....
3. ....
4. ....
5. ....

Episode Seven

Later that evening, someone on the ship makes a phone call to Marseilles.

"Can we meet in Barcelona tomorrow?"

"Barcelona tomorrow? Why? Why not here in Marseilles?"

"Someone was in my room today. I think they're watching me."

"What?"

"Don't worry. They didn't find the necklace. Look, do you want it or not?"

"What time do you arrive in Barcelona?"

"At eight o'clock tomorrow morning."

"All right. In Barcelona, call this number: 223-338."

Back in the lounge, Christina, Agatha, Lucy, Frank and Robert are having a drink.

"What do you want to do in Barcelona tomorrow, Aunt Agatha?"

"We can go to the museum, and maybe do some shopping later."

"What about you, Lucy?"

"I'm going to visit one of the fashion houses in the morning."

"And what about you, Frank?" asks Christina.

"I'm going to stay on the boat."

"Really? Why, Frank?" Lucy asks.

"I don't want to leave the book for a whole day. The writing's going well at the moment."

"Robert, you know Barcelona. Tell Frank how much there is to see."

"Well, there really is a lot—beautiful buildings, gardens, cafes, shops, restaurants, museums . . ."

"Sounds interesting. What are you going to do, Robert?"

"I have to contact my office about some houses near here. In the afternoon, Lucy and I are going to walk around."

"Frank, please come," Christina says. "Maybe you'll get some ideas for your book, and . . ."

"I'm too busy, really."

"Oh, Frank," says Agatha. "Come with us. We'll have a good time and you can explain to us the mysterious meanings of the paintings in the museum."

"All right, I'll go."

Meanwhile, in New York, Lieutenant Washington receives a telex.

"NECKLACE NOT IN ROOM/ SHIP STOPS IN BARCELONA TOMORROW/SUSPECT MAY TRY TO SELL IT THERE/WE NEED TO ACT SOON."

Washington says to his assistant, "So the necklace wasn't in the room. The suspect may try to sell it in Barcelona. We'd better contact Interpol."

Comprehension Check

1. Who makes a phone call to Marseilles? What is going to happen in Barcelona?
2. What are Christina and Agatha going to do in Barcelona?
3. What's Robert going to do?
4. Is Lucy going to spend the whole day with Robert?
5. At first, Frank doesn't want to leave the ship. Why?
6. Who searched the suspect's room? Why?

UNIT 8

Y: Hello, X?
X: Speaking.
Y: This is Y. I'm going to fly to Amsterdam next Monday. I'm going to stay at the Park Hotel. On Tuesday morning I'm going to meet you in the restaurant. We're going to begin Operation Eagle.
X: Very good. See you Tuesday.

Woman: Hello.
Control: Hello. Is 001 there?
Woman: Just a minute, please.
001: Hello.
Control: Hello, 001. This is Control. Could you come to my office right away? Enemy Agents X and Y are going to begin Operation Eagle next week. We need to stop them.
001: What are we going to do?
Control: I'm not sure yet.

Control: All right. Let's go over your assignments. Agent 001, what are you going to do next Monday?
001: At 6:30 AM I'm going to get to the airport. I'm going to drop off a package for 003 at the customs desk. Then at 7:05 AM I'm going to get on Y's plane and follow him to Amsterdam.
Control: 002?
002: I'm going to pick Agent 001 up at the airport in Amsterdam at 8:30 AM. We're going to follow Y to his hotel.
Control: Agent 003?
003: On Monday evening I'm going to pick up a package at the customs desk. Then I'm going to fly to Amsterdam. I'm going to check into Y's hotel. I'm going to put on my disguise there. Then I'm going to turn off the power at 10:00 PM.
Control: And then?
001, 002, 003: We're going to stop Operation Eagle.

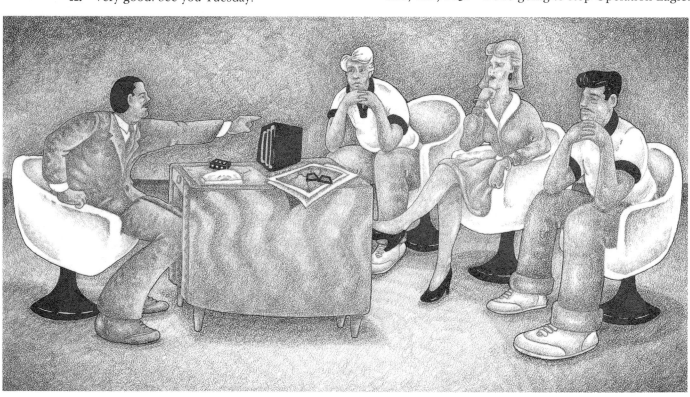

Speaking

1

Ask and answer questions about Agents 001, 002 and 003. Use these two- and three-word verbs:

Separable

pick up/drop off
put on/take off
turn on/turn off

Pick up *the letter.*
Pick *the letter* up.
Pick *it* up.

Inseparable

get on/get off
check into/check out of

Get on *the plane.*
Get on *it.*

At 6:30/001/package at the airport

A: At 6:30, is 001 going to pick up a package at the airport or drop it off?
B: He's going to drop it off.

1. At 6:30/001/package at the airport
2. At 7:05/001/Y's plane
3. In Amsterdam/001/Y's plane
4. At 8:30/002/Agent 001 at the airport
5. 003/Y's hotel
6. At Y's hotel/003/her disguise
7. At 10:00/003/the power in Y's hotel

2

Role-play these conversations.

Conversation 1:
A, you're 001. **B,** ask A "What're you going to do next Monday?"

Conversation 2:
B, you're 003. **A,** ask B "What're you going to do next Monday?"

3

Look at the pairs of pictures, and have conversations like this:

A: In picture four, what did the mother say?
B: "Take off your boots."
A: What did the children do?
B: They took them off.

Questions	Answers	
children	clean up	these words in the dictionary
wife	get on	your room
husband	look up	your boots
mother	pick up	me
father	take off	the bus
son	turn off	the stereo
daughter		
teacher		
students		

4

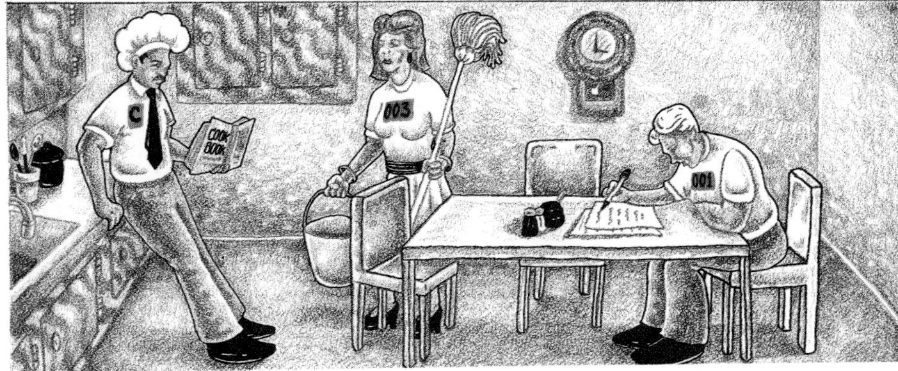

- Look at the picture and find these things:

cookbook	television (TV)	shopping list
vacuum cleaner	laundry bag	bucket

- Have conversations like this:

A: Who's reading a cookbook?
B: Control.
A: What's he going to do?
B: He's going to make dinner.

Questions	**Answers**	
turning on the TV	Control	go food shopping
reading a cookbook	001	watch TV
making a shopping list	002	make dinner
holding a vacuum cleaner	003	do the laundry
holding a bucket	Agent X	vacuum the bedroom
putting clothes in a laundry bag	Agent Y	wash the floor

- Ask each other questions like this:

A: Who usually does the laundry in your family?
B: I do. Who usually ....?

5

Pronunciation

Use the phrases below and have conversations like this:

A: Who's going to watch TV?

B: 002. Who's going to go grocery shopping?

go grocery shopping
watch TV
make dinner
do the laundry
vacuum the living room
wash the car

6

- Practice this conversation:

A: What're you going to do tomorrow night?
B: I'm going to go to the movies.
OR I'm not sure yet. Maybe I'll ....
OR I don't know yet.

- Have conversations like the one above. Use these times:

tonight
tomorrow morning/afternoon/night
this/year/Tuesday
next week/month/Saturday
on your next day off/birthday
after class

Here are some possible activities:

go to the movies
paint my apartment
go to Alaska
do my homework
visit friends
watch TV
....
....

- Ask each other about your plans for the weekend. Ask about people, places, times, etc.

7

Practice these telephone conversations:

Informal

A: Hello.
B: Hi, this is Bob. Is Alex there?
A: Yes, he is. Just a minute, please.
B: Thanks.

OR

A: Hello.
B: Hi, this is Bob. Is Alex there?
A: No, he isn't. Can I take a message?
B: Yes. Just tell him I called.
A: OK.
B: Thanks.
A and B: 'Bye.

Formal

B: Hello.
A: Hello. This is Bob Benton. May I please speak to Mrs. Ames?
B: Just a minute, please.
A: Thank you.

OR

B: Hello.
A: Hello. This is Bob Benton. May I please speak to Mrs. Ames?
B: She's not here right now. Can I take a message?
A: Could you tell her Bob Benton called, please?
B: All right.
A: Thank you.
A and B: Goodbye.

A

1. Make three calls. Call your friends Patty and Greg. Then call your teacher, Mrs. Morita.
2. B is going to call three times and ask for Susan, Alan and Mr. Johnson. Susan and Alan are home. Mr. Johnson isn't. You begin with *Hello.*

B

1. A is going to call three times and ask for Patty, Greg and Mrs. Morita. Patty and Mrs. Morita aren't home. Greg is. You begin with *Hello.*
2. Make three calls. Call your friends Susan and Alan. Then call your teacher, Mr. Johnson.

8
Culture Capsule

In most cities in the United States, you can dial a special telephone number for the following:

	all towns	some towns	your town
the weather		✓	
the time		✓	
the police	✓		
an ambulance	✓		
to report a fire	✓		
a joke		✓	
a prayer		✓	
a song		✓	
free financial advice		✓	

Can you phone for information like this in your town/city?

9
Put It Together

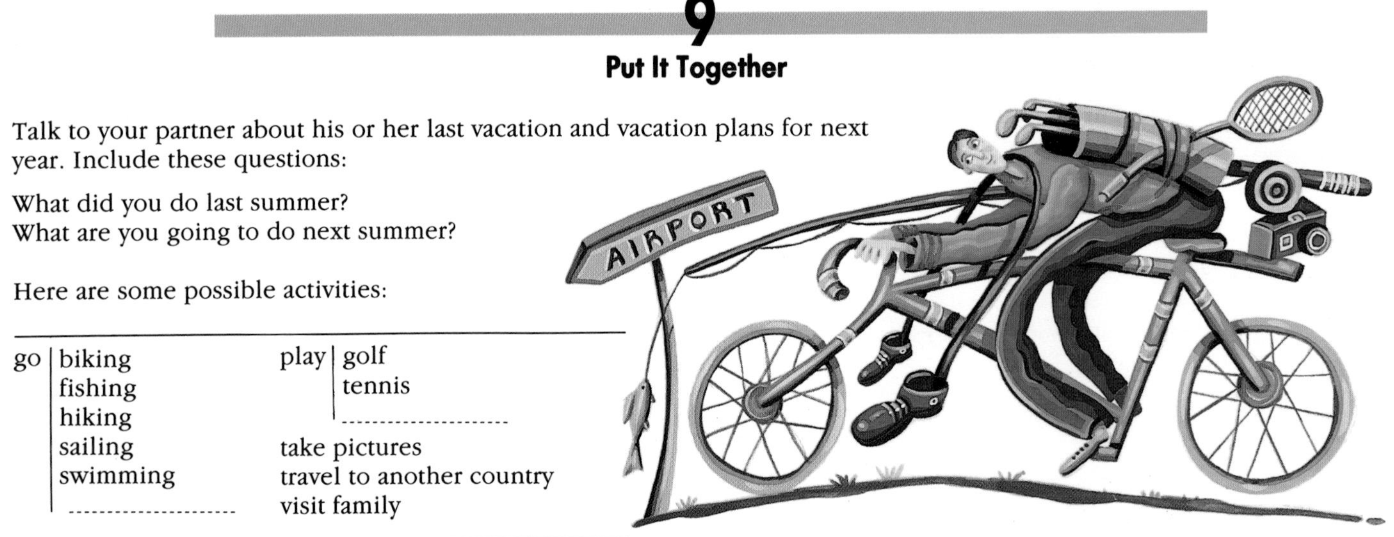

Talk to your partner about his or her last vacation and vacation plans for next year. Include these questions:

What did you do last summer?
What are you going to do next summer?

Here are some possible activities:

go | biking
fishing
hiking
sailing
swimming
----

play | golf
tennis
----

take pictures
travel to another country
visit family

I know how to . . .

CHECKLIST

USE THESE FORMS

☐ **Going To Future**

I	am	going to	leave in a minute.
He/She/It	is		
You/We/They	are		

questions

Is he going to get on the plane?
What is he going to do?

short answers

Yes, he is. No, he isn't.

statements

He is/isn't going to get on the plane.

☐ **Future Time Expressions**

tonight

tomorrow	morning
	afternoon
	night

this	weekend
next	month
	Saturday

on (your) next	day off
	vacation

☐ **Two- and Three-Word Verbs**

separable

Pick *the letter* up. Pick *it* up.
Pick up *the letter*. (Pick ~~up~~ *it*.)

clean up	put on
drop off	take off
look up	turn on
pick up	turn off

inseparable

Get on *the plane*. Get on *it*.
(Get *the* ~~*plane*~~ on.) (Get ~~*it*~~ on.)

check into	get on
check out of	get off

USE ENGLISH TO

☐ **ask for someone on the phone informally**
Hi, this is Bob. Is Alex there?

☐ **ask for someone on the phone formally**
Hello. This is Bob Benton. May I please speak to Mrs. Ames?

☐ **give and take a telephone message**
She's not here right now. Can I take a message?
Could you tell her I called, please?

☐ **talk about future plans**
What're you going to do tomorrow night?
I'm not sure yet. Maybe I'll go to the movies./I'm going to go to the movies.

☐ **talk about these subjects**
activities at home   weekend plans
vacation plans   telephone use

☐ UNDERSTAND THESE EXPRESSIONS

I'm not sure yet.
Just a minute, please.

do the laundry
make dinner
go on vacation
go over (an assignment)
right away
stay at (a hotel)
take a message

Listening

1

Listen to each dialogue. Check the correct box.

Someone:

1. ☐ is going to go grocery shopping.
   ☐ went grocery shopping.
2. ☐ is going to wash the car.
   ☐ washed the car.
3. ☐ is going to clean up the house.
   ☐ cleaned up the house.
4. ☐ is going to vacuum the living room.
   ☐ vacuumed the living room.
5. ☐ is going to pick up the kids.
   ☐ picked up the kids.

2

Read these suggestions:

Why don't you . . .?

a. put it on
b. turn it on
c. clean it up
d. look them up
e. turn it off
f. take it off

You're going to hear six conversations. Listen and decide which suggestion completes each conversation.

1. b
2. ....

3. ....
4. ....

5. ....
6. ....

3

These people are going to stay at the Park Hotel in Amsterdam this week: Elizabeth Taylor, Jane Fonda, Sean Penn and Paul McCartney. Which nights are they going to stay there? Write their names in the reservation book at the correct dates.

	MON 25	TUES 26	WED 27	THURS 28	FRI 29	SAT 30	SUN 31
		—	—	→			
					—	—	→
Sean Penn	—	—	—	—	→		
					—	→	

4

Part 1: You're going to hear five phone conversations. Some have messages, some don't. Check the correct box.

	Message	No Message
1.	☐	☐
2.	☐	☐
3.	☐	☐
4.	☐	☐
5.	☐	☐

Part 2: Now listen again and write down the messages. These are the names you're going to hear:

Terry Anderson
Mrs. Kister
Kathy
Sarah McCormack

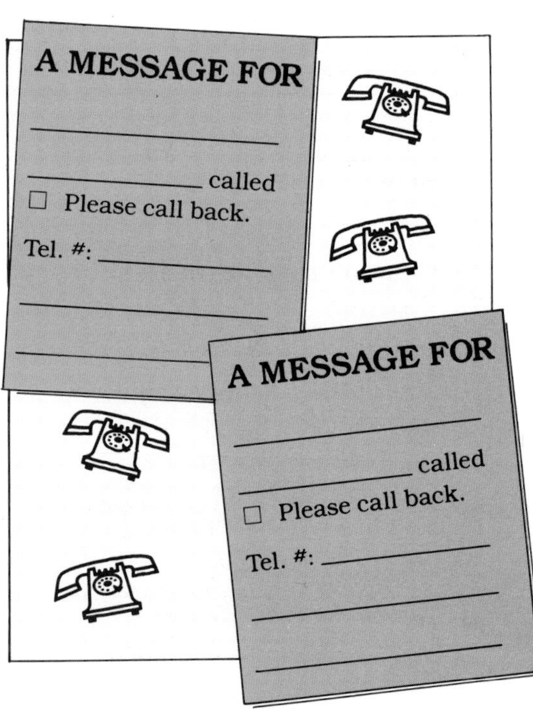

5

Give true answers.

1. ....
2. ....
3. ....
4. ....

Episode Eight

It is April 24. The ship is in Barcelona. Robert and Lucy are getting ready to leave the ship.

"Where are we going to meet this afternoon?" she asks.

Robert is thinking of something else but replies, "Oh. Uh. The Cafe Real at 2:00. It's the biggest cafe in the main square."

"OK, the Cafe Real. But can we meet before 2:00?"

"No, I have to see a few people this morning. Look, I have to hurry to make my first appointment. There's a taxi. I'll meet you in town, OK?"

Later that morning, Agatha, Christina and Frank stop at a cafe. They find a table outside. A waiter arrives and Frank orders two coffees and a tea in Spanish.

"I didn't know you spoke Spanish, Frank!" says Agatha.

"I can order coffee in lots of different languages."

"Is this your first visit to Spain?" Christina asks.

"No, about five years ago, we were here on vacation. It was spring . . . I was married. My wife died two years ago."

"Oh, I'm sorry, Frank."

There is a long silence. "Excuse me, I think I need a little walk."

In a phone booth near the cafe, someone is dialing 223-338. A man answers. "Very good, you're in Barcelona."

"Where are we going to meet?"

"At the Cafe del Comercio."

"I need directions."

"Where are you now?"

"Near the Plaza Real."

"Walk two blocks down Avenida Iberia and turn left on Rua Goya. It's in the middle of that block."

"Do you have the money?"

"Yes, of course."

It is now 2:00 PM. Lucy arrives at the Cafe Real to meet Robert. He is not there. She orders a coffee. The cafe is busy and she doesn't see the man watching her from the door of the cafe. Finally Robert arrives. The man at the door sees him and leaves.

"Sorry I'm late. . . ."

In the late afternoon, the passengers return to the ship. There is another telephone call to the man at 223-338.

"Where are you? Where is the necklace?"

"I'm back on the ship. Someone followed me. The necklace is in a safe place. Meet me in Malaga."

"I'm beginning to think you don't have it."

"Don't worry, I do."

"All right. We'll meet in Malaga. And bring the necklace."

Comprehension Check

1. In Barcelona, where are Lucy and Robert going to meet? When?
2. Is this Frank's first visit to Spain?
3. Why does Frank leave the cafe?
4. Who plans to meet at the Cafe del Comercio?
5. Why doesn't the meeting take place?
6. Do you know who watched Lucy? Do you know who followed the thief?

UNIT 9

Woman 1: Excuse me, how can I get downtown from here?
Woman 2: You can go by taxi, by bus or by local train.
Woman 1: How often do the buses run? Do you know?
Woman 2: Yes, every half hour.
Woman 1: How long does it take?
Woman 2: About forty-five minutes.

Woman 1: When's the next bus?
Clerk 1: There's one in ten minutes, at 12:30.
Woman 1: How much does it cost?
Clerk 1: One way is $6.50. Round trip is $12.
Woman 1: Then, I want to go to Milton. Do I have to change buses?
Clerk 1: Yes. Change at the downtown station.

Man: Can you suggest a good downtown hotel?
Clerk 2: You could try the Century. It's very nice.
Man: How much is it for two people?
Clerk 2: Let me see . . . $75 a night.

Speaking

1

A and **B,** ask and answer questions about the train schedule.

A: How often .... the trains run? Do you know?
B: Yes, before midnight ...., and after midnight ....
A: How long ....?
B: ....

LOCAL TRAINS

All trains go to Cambridgeport and Milton.
Change at downtown station for Rockport and Naperville.

Leave airport

6 a.m. – 12 midnight	every forty-five minutes
12 midnight – 6 a.m.	every two hours

Fare: $7.00 one way, $13.00 round trip

A.M.		P.M.	
Leave airport	Arrive downtown	Leave airport	Arrive downtown
12 midnight	12:35	12 noon	12:35
2:00	2:35	12:45	1:20
4:00	4:35	1:30	2:05
6:00	6:35	2:15	2:50
6:45	7:20	3:00	3:35
7:30	8:05	3:45	4:20

2

• Now look at the clock and ask about the next train.

B: When's ....?
A: There's one in ...., at ....
B: .... change for Cambridgeport?
A: ....
B: How much does it cost?
A: One way is ....

• **A,** ask about the next train. You want to go to Milton.

• **B,** ask about the next train. You want to go to Naperville.

3

Pronunciation

• Say items in a series like this: You can go by taxi, by bus or by local train.

• Look at the sentences below. **A,** your sentences are yellow. **B,** yours are blue. Find the questions and answers in your color. Add question marks (?) and periods (.).

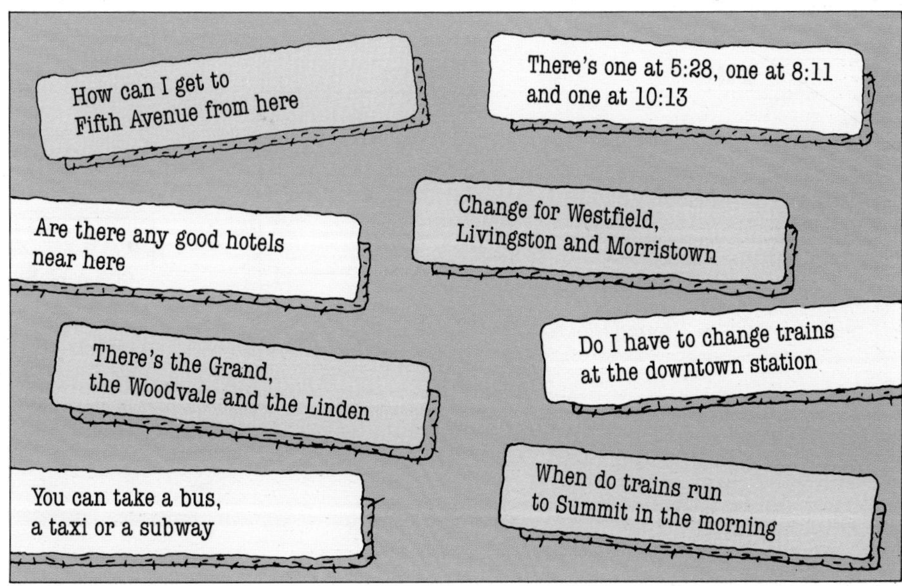

How can I get to Fifth Avenue from here
There's one at 5:28, one at 8:11 and one at 10:13
Are there any good hotels near here
Change for Westfield, Livingston and Morristown
There's the Grand, the Woodvale and the Linden
Do I have to change trains at the downtown station
You can take a bus, a taxi or a subway
When do trains run to Summit in the morning

• Now ask and answer the questions. **B,** answer A's questions and **A,** answer B's.

4

A and **B,** have conversations like this:

A: Excuse me, how .... Colesville from here?
B: You have to take .... There aren't any ....
A: When .... run?
B: At 8:43 AM, ... and ....
A: How long ....?
B: About ....
A: How much ....?
B: One way ....
A: .... change on the 8:43?
B: .... (Change at) ....

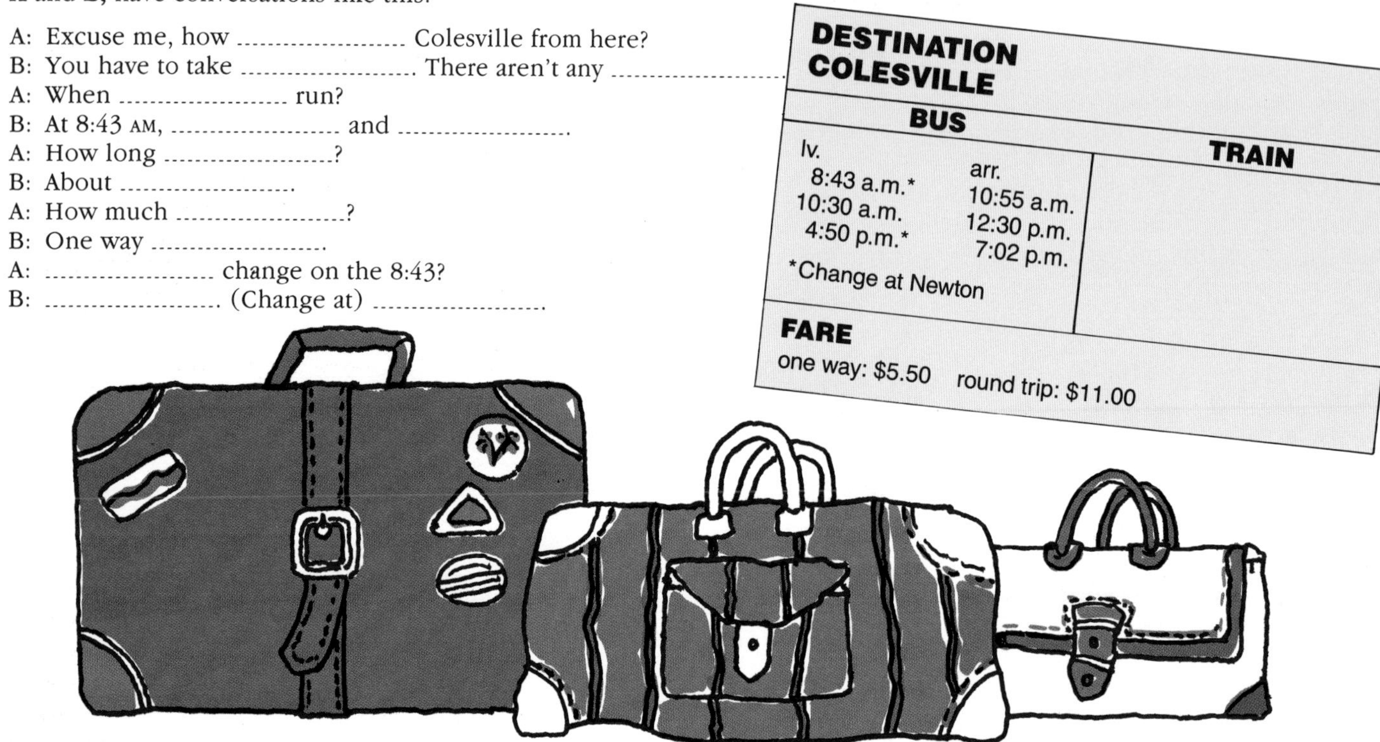

DESTINATION COLESVILLE

BUS		TRAIN
lv.	arr.	
8:43 a.m.*	10:55 a.m.	
10:30 a.m.	12:30 p.m.	
4:50 p.m.*	7:02 p.m.	
*Change at Newton		

FARE
one way: $5.50 round trip: $11.00

A

1. Ask B about Greenville.
2. Answer B's questions about Libertyville.

DESTINATION LIBERTYVILLE

BUS		TRAIN
lv.	arr.	
3:31 a.m.	7:31 a.m.	
6:16 a.m.*	10:30 a.m.	
2:27 p.m.*	6:45 p.m.	
*Change at Unionville		

FARE
one way: $12.25 round trip: $24.50

B

1. Answer A's questions about Greenville.

DESTINATION GREENVILLE

BUS	TRAIN	
	lv.	arr.
	9:06 a.m.*	12:00 p.m.
	11:17 a.m.*	2:23 p.m.
	7:48 p.m.	10:45 p.m.
	*Change at Balesville.	

FARE
one way: $8.50 round trip: $15.50

2. Ask A about Libertyville.

5

A and **B,** find out how your partner got to English class today/tonight.
Did he/she walk? Take a bus? A train? How long did it take? How much did it cost?

6

- Look at this subway map of Boston, and practice these conversations:

A: Excuse me, how can I get to the Aquarium?
B: Take the Orange Line to State. Then change to the Blue Line and go toward Wonderland. Get off at Aquarium. That's the next stop.
A: Thank you very much.

OR

A: Excuse me, how can I get to the Aquarium?
B: I'm sorry, I don't know.
A: Thank you anyway.

- **A,** ask about Government Center and Copley Square. **B,** ask about Harvard University and Symphony Hall.

Reproduced by Permission of MBTA, James F. O'Leary, General Manager

7

- Practice this conversation:

A: Can you suggest a good hotel in New York?
B: You could try the Plaza. It's very nice.
A: How much is it for one person/two people?
B: $300 a night/$500.
A: That's not bad. OR A: That's kind of expensive.
B: Well, you could try the Traveler's Inn. It's OK.

A

Ask B about hotels in Atlanta. Then answer B's questions about hotels in Orlando.

WHERE TO STAY IN ORLANDO

	one person	two people
High House	$130	$160
Harold Johnson's	$90	$125
Epcot Town House	$70	$90
Sunset Inn	$50	$70

B

Answer A's questions about hotels in Atlanta. Then ask A about hotels in Orlando.

WHERE TO STAY IN ATLANTA

	one person	two people
Atlanta Holton	$85	$115
Holly Inn	$65	$100
Center City Hotel	$45	$70
Carlson Hotel	$29	$40

- You're going to visit your partner's home town. Ask about hotels there.

8

Culture Capsule

In many places in the United States public transportation isn't very good. Not many trains or buses run from outside cities (the suburbs) to downtown. Most people have cars, and they like to drive. They drive to work, drive to go grocery shopping and drive their kids to school. Most people like to drive to work alone. There's a "rush hour" every morning from 7:01 to 8:59, and every evening from 4:30 to 7:30. In New York, the average commuter spends 81 minutes a day—or 310 hours a year—going to and from work!

Is public transportation in your country good? What kinds are there between cities? From outside cities to the downtown area? Inside cities? Do most people have cars? Do they drive to work? Do they drive alone or with other people? Are there rush hours? When are they?

9

Put It Together

Think about past trips to other cities or countries. Write down the name of one place and any information you remember. How long did you stay there? How did you get there? How long did the trip take? Did you stay in a hotel?

Ask your partner about his or her trip. Begin: *Where did you go? Were you on business or vacation?*

I know how to . . .

CHECKLIST

USE THESE FORMS

☐ **Have to** *(expresses need)*

questions
Do I have to change trains?

short answers
Yes, you do. No, you don't.

statements
You have to change at. . . .
You don't have to (change trains).

☐ **By**

You can go by | taxi.
bus.
train.
plane.

USE ENGLISH TO

☐ **ask for and give advice**
Can you suggest a good hotel?
You could try the Century.

☐ **suggest possibilities**
You can go by taxi, by bus or by local train.

☐ **ask for information about public transportation**
How often do the buses run? Do you know?
How long does it take?
How much does it cost?
Do I have to change buses for Milton?

☐ **hesitate**
Let me see. . . .

☐ **ask for and give directions**
Excuse me, how can I get to the Aquarium?
Take the Orange Line to State. Then change to . . . , and go toward . . . . Get off at . . . , the next stop.

☐ **talk about these subjects**
public transportation travel hotels

☐ UNDERSTAND THESE EXPRESSIONS

How much is it?

every two hours
one way
round trip

Listening

1

Sue Thompson is going to take a business trip to Nashville. Her assistant, Max Martin, makes two phone calls for her. He's new, and he makes a lot of mistakes. Correct Max's memos.

Part 1: Max calls the bus station.

Part 2: Max calls a travel agent.

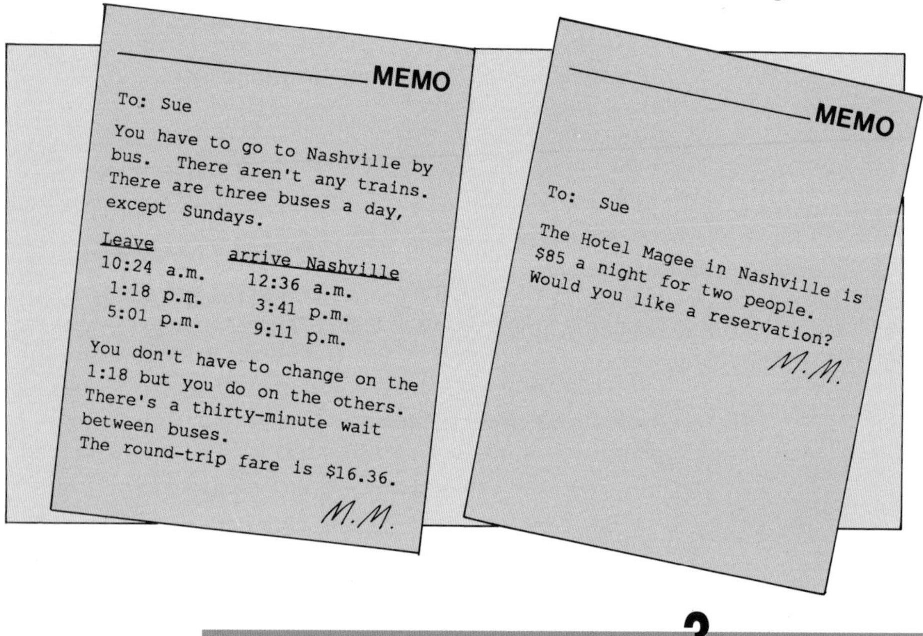

MEMO

To: Sue

You have to go to Nashville by bus. There aren't any trains. There are three buses a day, except Sundays.

Leave	arrive Nashville
10:24 a.m.	12:36 a.m.
1:18 p.m.	3:41 p.m.
5:01 p.m.	9:11 p.m.

You don't have to change on the 1:18 but you do on the others. There's a thirty-minute wait between buses.
The round-trip fare is $16.36.

M.M.

MEMO

To: Sue

The Hotel Magee in Nashville is $85 a night for two people.
Would you like a reservation?

M.M.

2

Complete the conversations. Choose *a* or *b*.

1. a. Yes, you can.
   b. You can take a taxi, a bus or a local train.
2. a. It takes half an hour.
   b. Every two hours, between 10:00 AM and 5:00 PM.
3. a. About 45 minutes.
   b. Every hour.
4. a. $4.50.
   b. That's kind of expensive.
5. a. One way.
   b. Yes, it is.
6. a. There aren't any others.
   b. No, you don't.
7. a. At 2:47.
   b. Yes, there is.
8. a. Every hour, between 6:00 AM and 9:00 PM.
   b. At 4:47.

3

Wilfred Klutz gets on a bus at Colesville. Listen and decide which picture describes his trip.

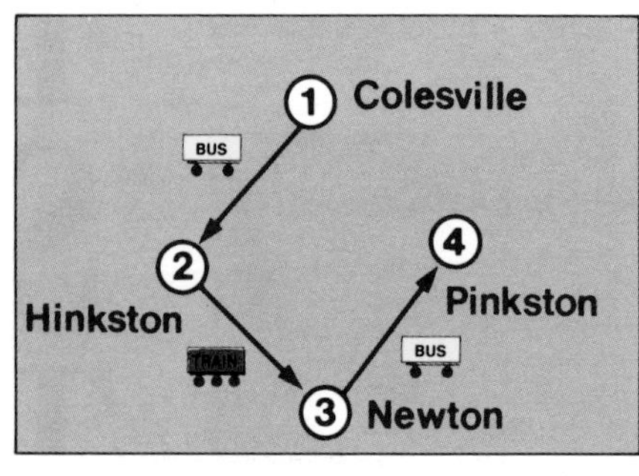

a. ___

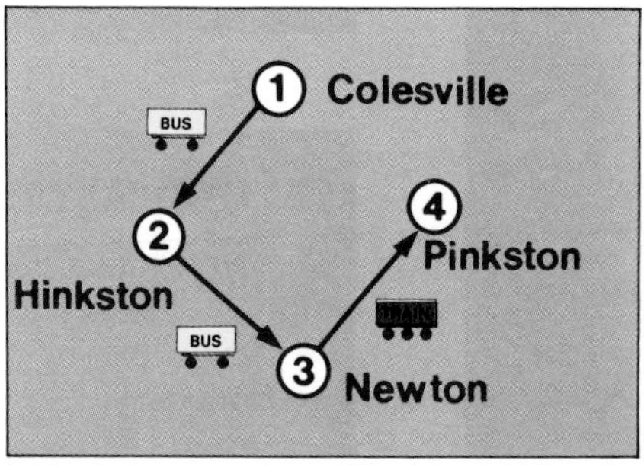

b. ___

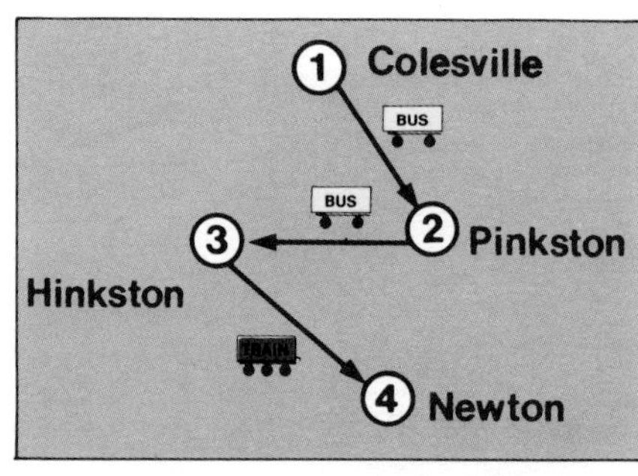

c. ___

4

Give true answers.

1. ....
2. ....
3. ....
4. ....

Episode Nine

It is April 25. Agatha is in her cabin. She's unpacking one of her suitcases to get her costume for the Costume Ball the next night. She takes out a long, dark blue dress, a mask and a hat the shape of the moon. She plans to go to the ball as the "Queen of the Night." She turns the dress around to look at it, and it brushes against the painting on the wall. The painting moves, and she sees something behind it. She looks more closely. It's a necklace! She takes the necklace from behind the painting and looks at it.

The Moon of India. From Christina's Museum, she thinks. Agatha sits down and puts her face in her hands. *What's the Moon of India doing here?* she thinks. *What should I do?* Then she gets up and puts the necklace in a small box. Quickly she walks to the purser's office.

"I want to put this in the ship's safe."

"Certainly, Madam. Please fill out this form."

Agatha fills out the form. The purser takes the box and puts it in the safe. He smiles as he gives Agatha a receipt.

"When do we arrive in Malaga?"

"The day after tomorrow, Madam, in the morning."

"Thank you very much," Agatha is only half listening.

"Is there anything else I can help you with?"

Agatha's mind is filled with questions, but she can't ask them now. "Well . . . not right now, thank you. Good night."

"Good night."

Christina returns to the cabin. It's almost dark. There's only a dim light on the table between the beds. Christina is very quiet. She thinks her aunt is asleep.

"Is that you, Christina?"

"You're still awake! Oh, I had a wonderful time talking with Frank. He's really an interesting man."

"That's nice, dear."

"Did you choose your costume?"

"What costume?"

"Your costume for the Costume Ball tomorrow night. Are you all right, Aunt Agatha?"

"Oh, I'm fine. Christina, did you ever see the Moon of India?"

"Yes. It's beautiful."

"What does it look like?"

"It's incredible. All diamonds and gold. It's . . . it's one of the most beautiful things in the world. I understand why somebody wanted to steal it."

"You do?"

"I'd love to have it. Well, I'm going to bed now. Good night, Aunt Agatha."

"Sleep well, my dear."

Comprehension Check

1. Is Agatha getting dressed for the Costume Ball?
2. What does she find behind the painting?
3. What does Agatha do with it?
4. What questions fill Agatha's mind?
5. Does Christina know a lot about the Moon of India?
6. Do you think Christina stole it?

UNIT 10

Begin Here
1
2
1st Street
Park
3
High Street
Main Street
2nd Street
4
SPEED LIMIT 25
3rd Street
Jays Book Store
5
THAI RESTAURANT
HARDWARE STORE
Park Street
4th Street
Drug Store
Shopping Center
STOP
ELLEN'S FLOWERS
5th Street
ACE Driving School
TWO HOUR PARKING
STOP
6th Street
6
No Parking
End Here

(1) **Driving Instructor:** All right, Mr. Klutz, that's enough for today. Why don't we go back to the driving school now?
Wilfred Klutz: OK. Uh, could you tell me where it is?
Instructor: It's on Park Street between 5th and 6th.
Klutz: Oh, yes, I remember. But how can I get there?
Instructor: Go straight ahead to the next light. Turn right on Main Street.

(2) **Instructor:** No, Mr. Klutz! You can't turn left here! You have to turn right. Right, turn right!

(3) **Instructor:** How fast are you going now, Mr. Klutz?
Klutz: 45.
Instructor: The speed limit here is 25 miles per hour.

(4) **Instructor:** Mr. Klutz! You just went through a red light!
Klutz: Sorry.

(5) **Instructor:** You'd better slow down, Mr. Klutz. There's another red light ahead. Look out for that car!
Klutz: Where do I go now?
Instructor: Go past the shopping center on your right. Then turn left at the next stop sign. The school's on the next corner, on the left.

(6) **Klutz:** Can I park here?
Instructor: No, you can't. You can park over there. And please do.

Speaking

1

Tell Mr. Klutz what these signs mean:

Don't turn left here.

1. 

2. NO TURNS

3. 

4. 

2

Tell Mr. Klutz another way to get to the driving school. Use these phrases to help you.

Turn left/right on (to) .... street.

Turn left/right at the next light/ corner/stop sign.

Go past .... on your left/right.

Go straight ahead (for .... blocks) (to ....).

Go to the next light/corner/stop sign.

3

A, give directions to a store on the map. Don't tell B the name of the place. **B,** follow A's directions until you get to the store. Which store is it?

4

Practice these conversations:

Peggy

A: Peggy looks pleased. What happened?
B: She just got a new car.
A: That's great!

Art

A: Art looks upset. What happened?
B: He just had a bad piano lesson.
A: That's too bad.

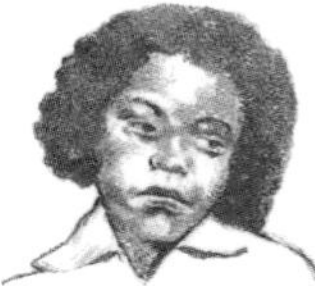

Ginny

Ricardo

Linda

Erik

Steve

Ann

A

1. Ask B about Ginny, Ricardo and Linda.
2. Answer B's questions about Steve, Ann and Erik: Steve just became a grandfather. Ann just got a letter from her boyfriend. Erik just had an accident with his car.

B

1. Answer A's questions about Ginny, Ricardo and Linda: Ricardo just found a new job. Ginny just heard some bad news. Linda just went to the dentist.
2. Ask A about Steve, Ann and Erik.

5
Pronunciation

- Practice saying the words below.

Say a noun + noun combination like this:
trȧvel agency   bȯokstore

coffee shop	furniture store	shoe store
post office	clothing store	drugstore
travel agency	bookstore	hardware store

- Ask and answer questions like this:

A: Where can you buy clothes?
B: At a clothing store.

clothes	paint	plane tickets
shoes	chairs	toothpaste and shampoo
stamps	books	

6

You and your partner just moved to new neighborhoods. Ask where you can buy things. Then ask your partner where the store is and find it on your map.

A: I have to buy some books. Where can I get them?
B: Why don't you go to The Bookseller?
A: Excuse me?
B: The Bookseller.
A: Could you tell me where it is?
B: It's on Drew Road across from the movie theater.
A: Oh, it's number 3 on the map.

on the corner of .... and ....
next to ....
on the left
on the right
between .... and ....
across from ....

A

1. You want to buy these things:

chairs, stamps, shoes, vegetables, traveler's checks

Ask B where you can buy them. Then find the store on your map.

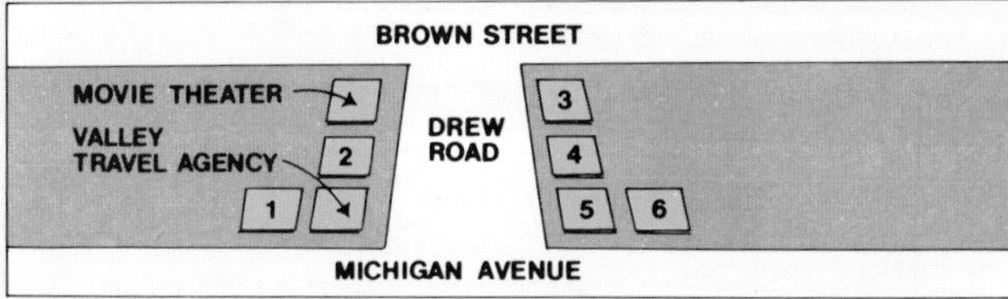

2. Answer B's questions. Use your map and the key below.

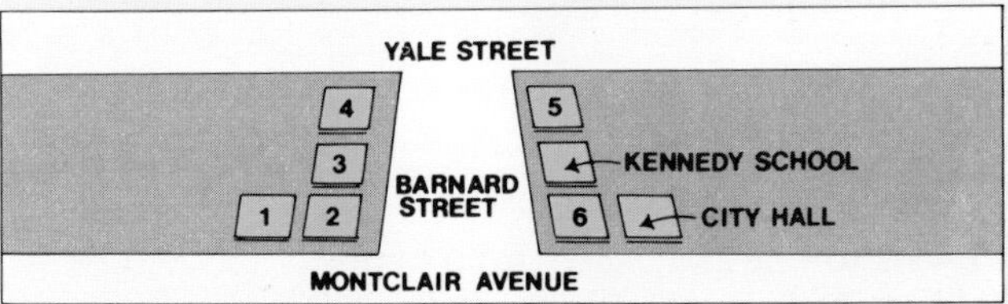

Key to map:
1. Michaels Men's Clothing
2. Betty's Bakery
3. Ellen's Flowers
4. Lucas Drugstore
5. Robert's Hardware
6. Diane's Clothing for Women

B

1. Answer A's questions. Use your map and the key below.

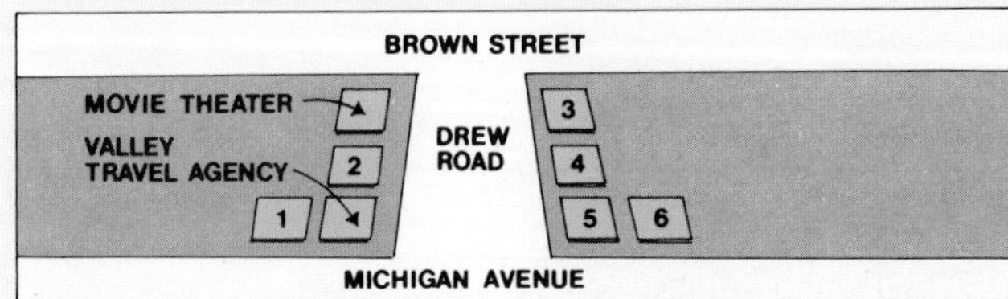

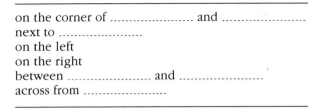

Key to map:
1. Emerson's Furniture
2. the post office
3. The Bookseller
4. Third National Bank
5. Miller's Shoe Store
6. P and A Grocery

2. You want to buy these things:

paint and paintbrushes, flowers, toothpaste and shampoo, clothes, bread and rolls

Ask A where you can buy them. Then find the store on your map.

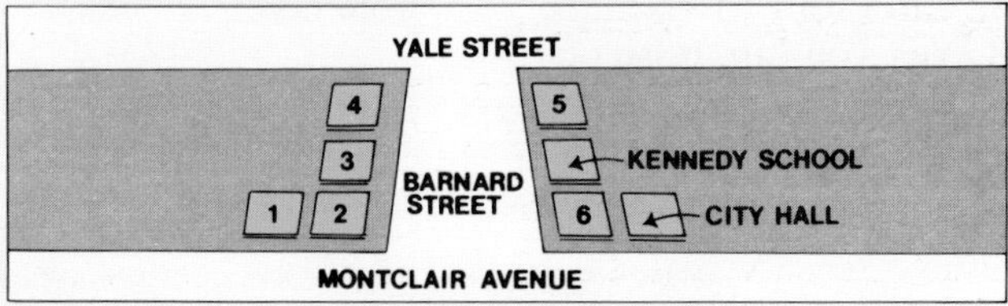

7

Pronunciation

Say an adjective + noun combination like this: local train red light German restaurant

Practice saying these restaurant and street names:

The Little Chef The Hunan Palace Atlantic Avenue Little Tokyo Tuscan Kitchen Pacific Avenue

8

- Ask your partner about restaurants in your new neighborhood.

A: Is there an Indian restaurant near here?
B: Yes, there are two. There's one on Kentucky Road and another on North Carolina Drive.
A: Is there a Brazilian restaurant?
B: I'm sorry. I don't know.

INDIAN	
Bengal Tiger	10 Kentucky Road
Nirvana	5 North Carolina Drive

A

1. Ask B about these kinds of restaurants. Then listen and check the correct box.

	one	two	?
Italian	☐	☐	☐
Japanese	☐	☐	☐
Spanish	☐	☐	☐

2. Answer B's questions. Use this guide:

CHINESE	
The Hunan Palace	5 Pacific Ave.
The Jade Garden	17 Virginia Ave.
FRENCH	
The Little Chef	2 Indiana Ave.
GREEK	
The Acropolis	550 Park Place
Spiro's	77 Connecticut Ave.

B

1. Answer A's questions. Use this guide:

ITALIAN	
Tuscan Kitchen	223 Mediterranean Ave.
Caesar's	600 Tennessee Ave.
JAPANESE	
Atlantic Sushi	115 Atlantic Ave.
Little Tokyo	52 New York Road
MEXICAN	
Manuel's	33 Vermont St.

2. Ask A about these kinds of restaurants. Then listen and check the correct box.

	one	two	?
Chinese	☐	☐	☐
Russian	☐	☐	☐
French	☐	☐	☐

- **A,** choose three restaurants you would like to go to. Ask B how far they are.
B, you decide if A can walk or needs to take a cab.

A: Can I walk to .... from here?
B: Yes, you can. It isn't far.

OR

A: Can I walk to .... from here?
B: You'd better take a taxi. It's pretty far.

9

Put It Together

A, you're at B's house. You want to buy shoes, a jacket, and ....
B is going to go with you. Then you want to take B out to dinner.
You will take public transportation.

Ask B questions like these. **B,** give true information.
Where can I buy ....?
How can we get there?
Where can we go for dinner?

I know how to . . .

CHECKLIST

USE THESE FORMS

☐ **Imperative**

Go straight ahead to the next light.
Don't turn left here.

☐ **One/Another**

Is there *an Indian restaurant* near here?
Yes, there's *one* on Kentucky Road and *another (one)* on North Carolina Drive.

USE ENGLISH TO

☐ **make suggestions**
Why don't you go back to the driving school?

☐ **give strong advice**
You'd better slow down.

☐ **talk about rules**
You can't turn left here. You have to turn right.

☐ **talk about needs**
I have to buy some books.

☐ **ask for and give locations**
Could you tell me where it is?
It's on Park Street between 5th and 6th.

☐ **ask for and give directions**
How can I get there?/Where do I go now?
Go straight ahead to the next light.
Turn right on Main Street.

☐ **respond to good or bad news**
That's great!
That's too bad.

☐ **talk about these subjects**
directions driving regulations
neighborhoods stores restaurants

☐ UNDERSTAND THESE EXPRESSIONS

The speed limit here is 25 miles per hour.
Look out for that car!
You just went through a red light.

shopping center
no parking
over there
slow down

Listening

1

Look at the picture and listen to the information. Is the information true or false? Write *T* or *F*.

1. ___
2. ___
3. ___
4. ___
5. ___
6. ___

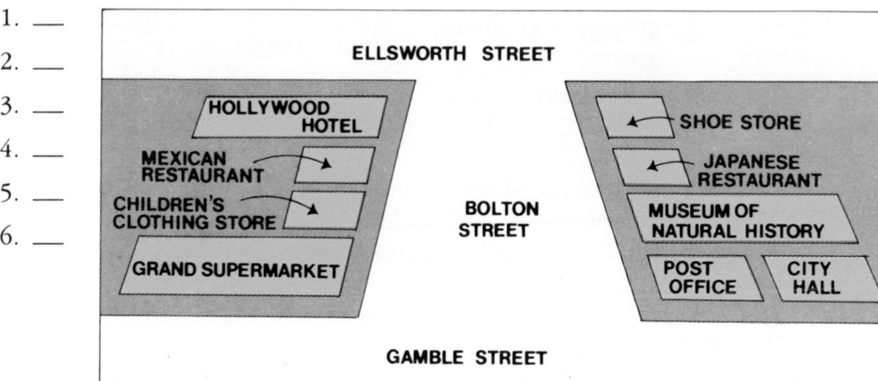

2

This is a map of Greenwich Village. You're going to hear three people ask for directions. Follow the directions to each place and write the number of the conversation in the circle. (Each person begins at 5th Avenue, between 8th and 9th Street.)

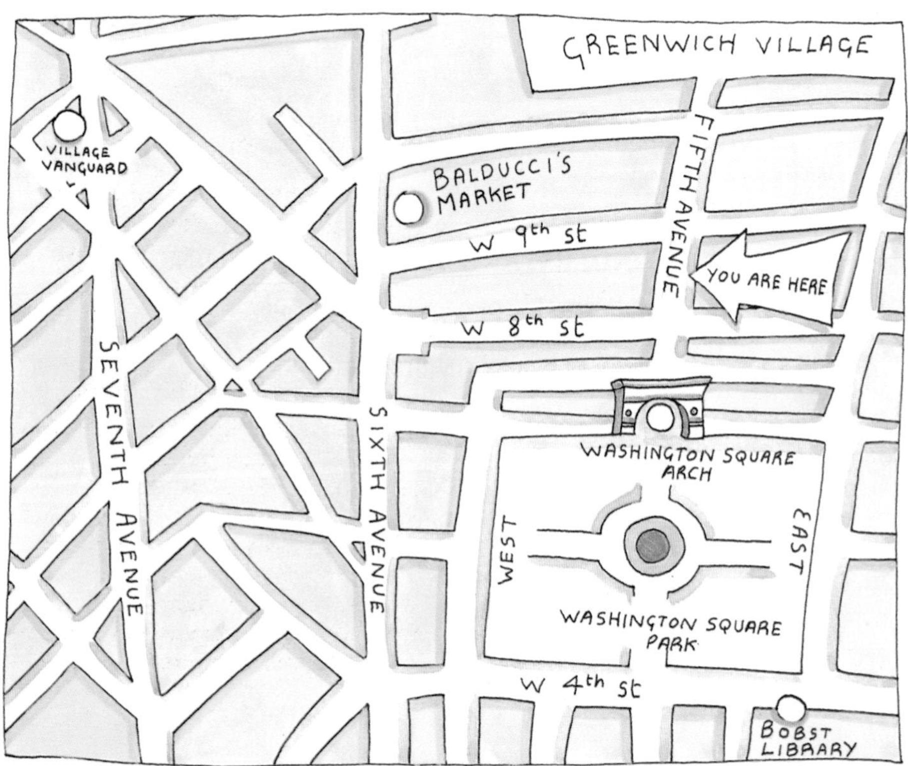

3

Listen to the five short conversations. Number the traffic signs in the correct order, 1–5.

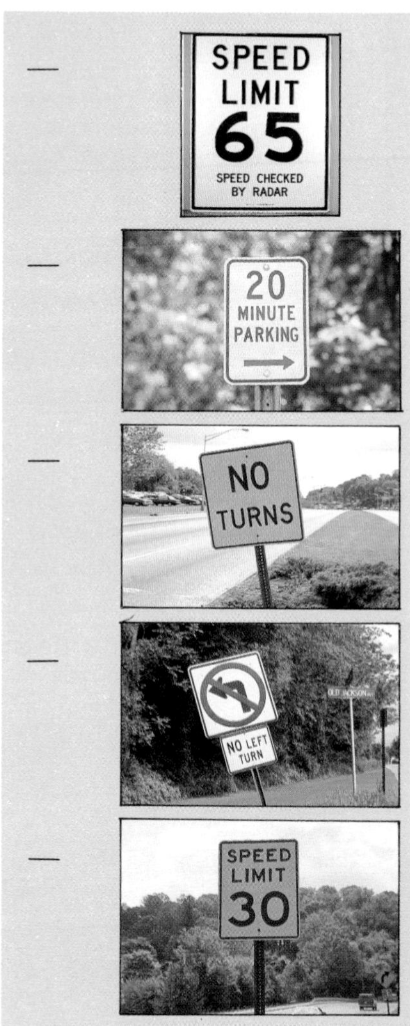

4

Give true answers.

1. ....
2. ....
3. ....
4. ....

Episode Ten

The next evening Christina and Agatha are sitting in the lounge, just outside the ballroom where the music and dancing are beginning. Christina is wearing a Cleopatra costume. Agatha smiles as she looks at Christina. *A beautiful woman,* she thinks. *Could she possibly . . . ?*

A man wearing a hat and a trench coat enters the lounge. He looks like a spy.

"Is that Frank?" asks Christina. "Frank!" she calls.

Frank replies in a deep voice, "Sorry darling, guess again."

"James Bond!" says Agatha.

Frank looks at the two women. He continues in his deep voice, "Now, let me guess. Christina, you're the beautiful Cleopatra, Queen of Egypt, and you, Agatha, you're. . . ."

"The Queen of the Night."

"Of course. You both look wonderful."

Robert, in a waiter's uniform enters carrying a tray of drinks. The others don't see his face, only his white uniform and the drinks.

"Compliments of the Captain."

"That's very nice." Christina then sees it is Robert and laughs.

"Robert, where did you get that costume?"

"One of the waiters. I gave him ten dollars to borrow it. It looks good on me, don't you think?" He spills a drink on Agatha's dress. "Oh Agatha, I'm sorry."

"Don't worry, Robert. Excuse me, I'll just go and put some water on it."

Agatha walks down the hall. She opens the door to the ladies' room and sees someone wearing a man's suit. "Oh, excuse me," and she begins to go out.

"Agatha. It's all right. It's me, Lucy."

"Lucy!"

"It's my Al Capone gangster suit."

Lucy's jacket is open, and while she is looking in the mirror, Agatha sees that she is carrying a gun. The gun looks real and Agatha is frightened.

"It's a very nice costume, dear, very realistic," Agatha says.

In the ballroom, people are dancing. Robert, Christina and Frank are standing by the door.

"Where's Lucy?" Robert asks.

"I didn't see her," Christina replies.

"Maybe she's dancing. You see the woman in the black mask? Is that Lucy?" Frank suggests.

Robert wants to take a closer look, and invites Christina to dance. There are many people on the dance floor. The music and dancing continue for hours.

While most people are enjoying the ball, one person quickly enters the Jordans' cabin, looks behind the painting for the necklace, doesn't find it, throws the painting down and leaves the cabin.

Comprehension Check

1. Why do you think Christina chose a Cleopatra costume?
2. Who does Frank look like?
3. Is Robert a good waiter?
4. Does Agatha meet a man in the ladies' room?
5. Why is Agatha frightened?
6. Who throws down the painting in Agatha and Christina's room? Why?

UNIT 11

Chuck: Good afternoon, folks. I'm Chuck. What are you looking for? What kind of car do you like?
George: Well, I like a big car.
Martha: I don't really agree with my husband. I like small ones better.
Chuck: What do you like about them?
Martha: Smaller cars are more economical.
George: Bigger cars are more comfortable.
Chuck: Well, in general I agree with both of you. We have lots of popular models. We'll find the right one for you.
George: Which one is the most powerful?
Martha: Which one is the cheapest?

(later) . . .
George: Well, Martha, which one do you like?
Martha: I don't know, George. The two-door is the cheapest, and it gets better mileage than the others. It *is* the most economical. What do *you* think of it?
George: I think it's too slow and too uncomfortable, and it isn't powerful enough. Now, the four-door is bigger, faster, more—
Martha: Expensive.
George: That's OK. We can afford it. After all, you only live once.
Martha: In that case, do you know which one I *really* like? The sports car.
George: Martha, I love you. I really want the sports car, too. Young man? Chuck? We'll take the Cheetah!

	The Cheetah	The Leo	The Cat
price	$18,190	$12,400	$8,678
weight	2900 lbs.	3200 lbs.	2400 lbs.
0-60 m.p.h.	6 secs.	18 secs.	16 secs.
miles per gallon	14	22	28
seating capacity	2	6	4

Speaking

1

Note:

1 lb. (pound)	=	.45 kilograms
60 seconds	=	1 minute
1 mile	=	1.6 kilometers
1 gallon	=	3.8 liters

- Ask and answer questions comparing two models:

A: Which is heavier, the two-door or the four-door?
B: The four-door. Which one ....?

Use these words:

expensive – cheap	fast – slow
heavy – light	big – small

- Ask and answer questions comparing three models:

A: Which one is the fastest?
B: The sports car. Which one ....?

2

Which do you think are better, big cars or small cars? Agree or disagree with your partner. Give reasons. Use these words:

powerful	economical
cheap	(un)comfortable

A: I think small cars are better. They .... than big cars.
B: I agree. Big cars are too ....

OR I don't agree. Small cars are too ....
They're not .... enough.
Big cars are .... than small cars.

3

Practice reading this out loud.

1. The three tallest mountains are Everest, Kanchenjunga and K2.
2. The three largest islands are New Guinea, Borneo and Greenland.
3. The three biggest lakes are Lake Superior, Lake Victoria and the Caspian Sea.
4. The three longest rivers are the Mississippi, the Nile and the Amazon.

Note:

1 sq. mi. (square mile) = 259 hectares
1 ft. (foot) = .305 meters

1,000 = one thousand
1,000,000 = one million
1,000,000,000 = one billion

A

The Three Tallest Mountains
Everest (Asia)
Kanchenjunga (Asia)
K2 (Asia)

The Three Largest Islands
New Guinea (South Pacific)
Borneo (South Pacific)
Greenland (North America)

Lakes
Lake Superior 31,820 sq. mi.
Lake Victoria 26,828 sq. mi.
The Caspian Sea 170,000 sq. mi.

Rivers
The Mississippi 3,872 mi. (long)
The Nile 4,145 mi. (long)
The Amazon 4,000 mi. (long)

1. Ask B questions to find out the tallest mountain and the largest island. For example: *What's the tallest mountain in the world?* Write 1 next to the answers.
2. Answer B's questions.
3. Ask B questions about the other two mountains and islands. For example: *Which is taller, Everest or K2?* Mark the answers 2 and 3.
4. Answer B's questions.

B

Mountains
Everest 29,108 ft. (tall)
Kanchenjunga 28,208 ft. (tall)
K2 28,268 ft. (tall)

Islands
New Guinea 317,000 sq. mi.
Borneo 287,000 sq. mi.
Greenland 840,000 sq. mi.

The Three Biggest Lakes
Lake Superior (North America)
Lake Victoria (Africa)
The Caspian Sea (Asia/Europe)

The Three Longest Rivers
The Mississippi (North America)
The Nile (Africa)
The Amazon (South America)

1. Answer A's questions.
2. Ask A questions to find out the biggest lake and the longest river. For example: *What's the biggest lake in the world?* Write 1 next to the answers.
3. Answer A's questions.
4. Ask A questions about the other lakes and rivers. For example: *Which is bigger, Lake Superior or Lake Victoria?* Mark the answers 2 and 3.

4

- Have conversations about these pictures.

these shoes/small/wear

A: What's the matter? OR What's wrong?
B: These shoes are too small.
I can't wear them.

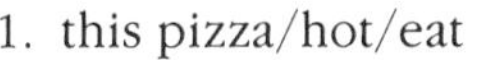

1. this pizza/hot/eat

2. this sofa/heavy/move

3. these gloves/ expensive/afford

- Have conversations about these pictures.

keep up with/those people/fast

A: What's wrong? OR What's the matter?
B: I can't keep up with those people.
I'm not fast enough.

1. see/that movie/old

2. reach/those cookies/ tall

3. figure out/ that problem/smart

5

Ask your partner these questions. Agree or disagree with his/her answers.

A: What do you think? Which is more enjoyable, a vacation at the ocean or a vacation in the mountains?
B: A vacation in the mountains.
A: I agree (with you). Which ....?
OR I don't really agree (with you). I think a vacation at the ocean is more enjoyable. Which ....?

1. Which is better, hot weather or cold weather?
2. Which is the easiest, chemistry, biology or psychology?
3. Who's more famous, Elvis Presley or James Dean?
4. Who's smarter, men or women?
5. Which is more important, an interesting job or a good salary?

- Use these words and make up your own questions:

	good	*bad*
good bad	good better best	bad worse worst

	healthy
healthy funny easy	healthy healthier healthiest

	rich
rich hot old small	rich richer richest

	beautiful
beautiful comfortable interesting popular	beautiful more beautiful most beautiful

6

Ask your partner his/her opinion on these questions. Agree or disagree.

A: Who's the best tennis player in the world?
B: I think it's ....
A: I think so, too.
OR Really? I don't think so. I think it's ....

1. What's the fastest car?
2. .... popular song in your country right now?
3. .... famous man/woman from your country?
4. .... powerful person in the world?
5. ....?

7

Culture Capsule

Sports are very popular in the United States, both to watch and to play. The most popular sports to watch are: football, baseball, basketball, bowling, golf and tennis.

What are the most popular sports in your country?
Which sports do you like to watch?
Which sports do you like to play?

8

Put It Together

A, B and **C,** you each want to buy a house.

A, you have three children. You can afford to pay $130,000.

B, you're single. You have a lot of money. You collect modern art. You can afford to pay $500,000.

C, you and your wife/husband are retired. Your children are married and don't live with you anymore. You like to garden. You can afford to pay $120,000.

old – new	modern – old-fashioned
big – small	interesting – boring
attractive – ugly	expensive – cheap

- Ask your partners these questions. Use the words above to help you.

Which house do you like best?
What do you like about it?
Why do you like it better than the others?

- Ask the same questions, but give true answers.

I know how to . . .

USE THESE FORMS

☐ **Adjective Comparisons**

To compare two things use the comparative.
Small cars are faster than big cars.
Big cars are more expensive than small cars.

To compare three or more things, use the superlative.
The two-door is the cheapest of all the cars here.
It isn't the most comfortable.

Add -er *or* -est *to adjectives of one syllable* (tall taller tallest) *or adjectives ending in* -y (easy easier easiest).

Spelling

Words ending in -y *change the* y *to* i *before adding* -er *or* -est.
easy easier easiest

Words ending consonant-vowel-consonant double the final consonant.
big bigger biggest

Use more *or* most *before words of three or more syllables* (more powerful) *or words of two syllables not ending in* -y (most modern).

irregular comparisons
good better best
bad worse worst

☐ **Too/Enough**

It's too slow and uncomfortable, and it isn't powerful enough.
This pizza is too hot. I can't eat it.

USE ENGLISH TO

☐ **ask someone's opinion**
What kind of car do you like?
What do you like about them?
Which one do you like?

☐ **give an opinion**
I like big cars. Bigger cars are more comfortable.
I think it's too slow.

☐ **agree**
I agree (with you)./I think so, too.

☐ **disagree**
I don't really agree with you.
Really? I don't think so. I think . . . .

☐ **show concern**
What's the matter?/What's wrong?

☐ **talk about these subjects**
speed weight size quantity
large numbers cars sports
geography houses

☐ UNDERSTAND THESE EXPRESSIONS

Good afternoon.
It gets good mileage.
That's OK.
We can afford (to buy) it.
You only live once.

after all
in general
in that case
miles per gallon

CHECKLIST

Listening

1

Listen to the conversation and check the correct answer.

1. Which is smaller?
   ___ Monaco ___ San Marino

2. Which is faster?
   ___ an antelope ___ a cheetah

3. Which is taller?
   ___ Sears Tower
   ___ the World Trade Center

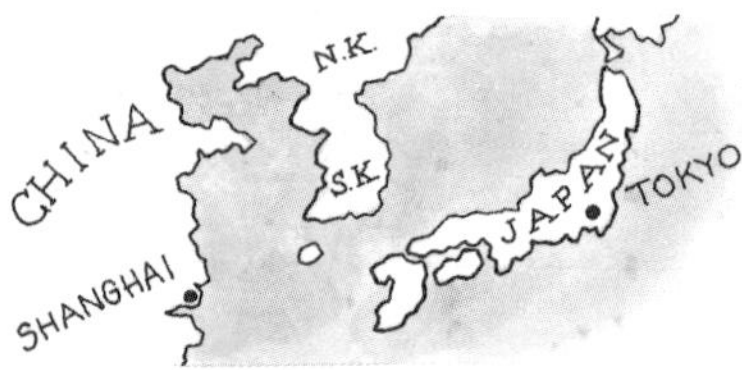

4. Which has the biggest population?
   ___ Shanghai ___ Tokyo

5. Which is the heaviest animal?
   ___ a hippopotamus
   ___ an elephant

2

Which picture is correct, according to the conversation? Circle *a* or *b*.

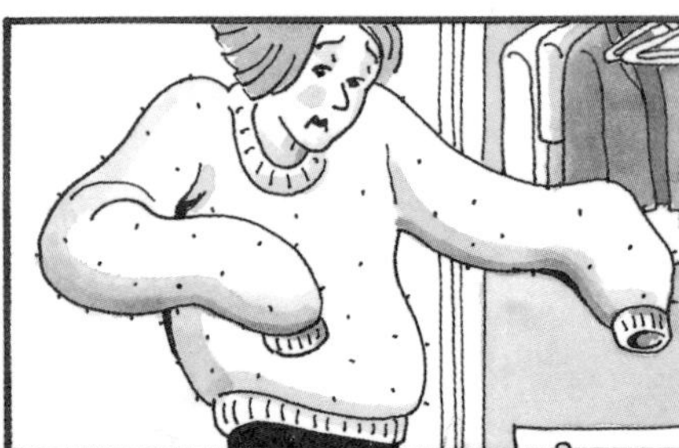

1. a. b.

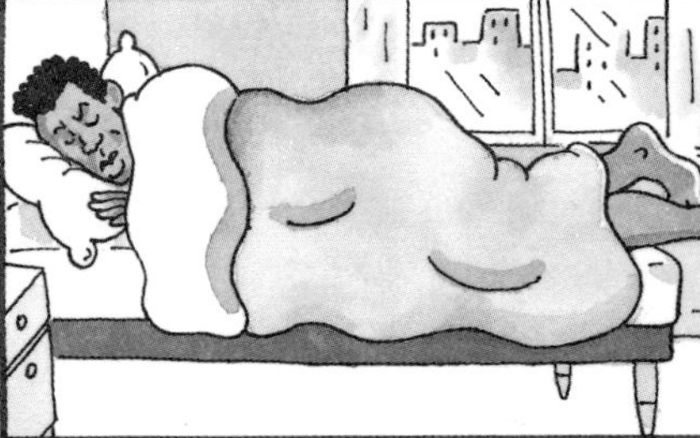

2. a. b.

3. a. b.

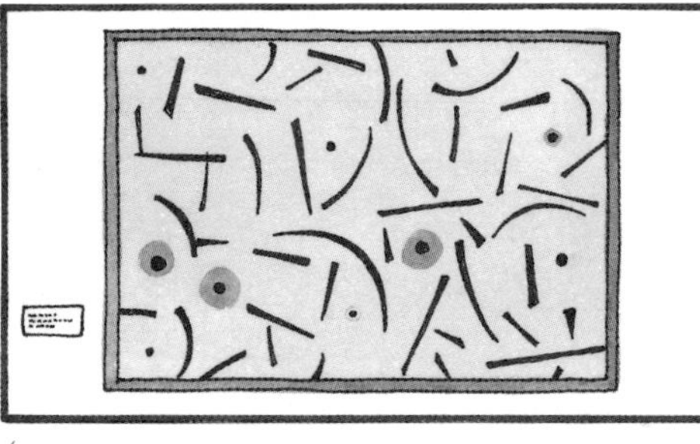

4. a. b.

3

Give true answers.

1. .... 2. ....

3. .... 4. ....

MOON OF INDIA

Episode Eleven

Agatha leaves the ball and returns to her cabin. She sees the painting on the floor. She stands for a moment in the doorway. Suddenly, there is somebody behind her. Agatha screams and then sees it is Lucy.

"What's the matter, Agatha?"

"Somebody was in here."

"You should. . . ."

"Please. I think you know about this."

"Agatha, what are you talking about?"

"You're not a fashion buyer. I know that. Pierre Maurice, the designer we talked about the first night, died ten years ago. And why are you carrying a gun? I saw a gun under your jacket this evening."

"It's part of my costume."

"And you put the Moon of India in our room. But you won't get it back."

"I am looking for the necklace, Agatha. You see, I'm a police officer." She shows Agatha her police identification card. "I'm on this cruise to find the necklace and arrest the person who stole it."

"But if you're not the thief, Lucy, who is?"

On deck, Robert and Christina are talking. "Your job must be very interesting, Christina."

"Yes it is. The City Museum has one of the best Egyptian collections in the country."

"And it had the Moon of India."

"Yes, it was magnificent."

"It still is magnificent."

"Yes, of course. It still is magnificent, wherever it is."

They watch the ocean and the stars. Robert takes Christina's arm. "Would you like to come to my cabin and have a drink?"

"It's a little late, Robert."

"I'm leaving early tomorrow. This is my last night. Let's just have one drink."

"All right, but I can't stay long."

Comprehension Check

1. What does Agatha think when she sees the painting on the floor?
2. How does Agatha know that Lucy is not a fashion buyer?
3. At first, does Agatha think Lucy stole the necklace? Why?
4. How does Agatha learn that Lucy is a police officer?
5. What are Robert and Christina talking about on the deck?
6. Why does Robert invite Christina to his cabin?

UNIT 12

Rick: Hi, Jane. What's wrong? You look depressed.
Jane: Hello, Rick. I just filled out a questionnaire in this magazine. I'm a boring person.
Rick: No, you're not. Why do you say that?
Jane: Well, for example, which do you like better, Walt Disney or James Bond movies?
Rick: That's easy. James Bond movies. In fact, Sean Connery's my favorite actor. Who's yours?
Jane: Mine's Woody Allen, and I like Walt Disney movies. Where do you like to eat out?
Rick: At any foreign restaurant, I guess. I like to try new things.
Jane: Would you rather watch TV or go out in the evening? I'd rather watch TV.
Rick: Really? I'd rather go out.
Jane: See? I'm boring. What do you think? Will your life be different in five years?
Rick: Probably. I hope so anyway. What about you?
Jane: Probably not. I'll have the same job, live in the same place. . . . What would you like to do for your next vacation?
Rick: I don't know. I'd **like** to go to an exciting place, like the Amazon or Mt. Everest.
Jane: Do you think you will?
Rick: I doubt it, but maybe someday. You've got to have dreams.

ARE YOU BORING OR EXCITING?
Do you agree with these statements?
Answer Yes or No.
YES 1. I like Walt Disney movies better than James Bond movies.
NO 2. I like James Bond movies better than Walt Disney movies.
YES 3. I like to eat out at McDonald's and Burger King.
NO 4. I like to eat out at foreign restaurants.
YES 5. I'd rather watch TV than go out in the evening.
NO 6. I'd rather go out than watch TV in the evening.
YES 7. My life probably won't change very much in five years.
NO 8. Maybe someday my life will be completely different.
YES 9. For my next vacation, I'd like to stay home and rest.
NO 10. For my next vacation, I'd like to go to an unusual place like Antarctica.
SCORING:
For 1, 3, 5, 7, and 9, give yourself 2 points for each No and 1 point for each Yes.
For 2, 4, 6, 8, and 10, give yourself 2 points for each Yes and 1 point for each No.
Is your score 16-20? You're an exciting person!
Is your score 10-15? You're boring! You need help!

Speaking

1

A, ask Jane's questions. **B,** give true answers. Then figure out your scores.

2

- Have conversations like these. Use *Who* for people. Use *What* for things.

A: Who's your favorite actress?
B: Meryl Streep.
A: She's mine, too.

OR

A: Who's your favorite actress?
B: I don't have one. Who's yours?
OR Jessica Lange. Who's yours?
A: Mine's ....

actor	book	color	singer
actress	sport	movie	

- Find out the favorites of other people in your class. Then ask and answer questions about them.

A: Who are Arturo's and Alicia's favorite actresses?
B: His is Joan Collins. Hers is Elizabeth Taylor.

my -	....
your -	....
his -	....
her -	....
our -	ours
their -	theirs

3

Listen to music

classical *Bach, Mozart*
popular *John Denver, Billy Joel*
jazz *Ella Fitzgerald, Dizzy Gillespie*

Play sports

basketball tennis baseball

Go to movies

cartoons *Mickey Mouse*
westerns *The Good, the Bad and the Ugly*
thrillers *Psycho*

• Ask your partner what he/she likes. Have conversations like these:

A: Do you like to listen to music?
B: Yes, I do.
A: What kind of music do you like?
B: ....

OR

A: Do you like to listen to music?
B: Not especially. Do you?
A: ....

• Have conversations like this:

A: Would you rather listen to music or play sports?
B: I'd rather play sports (than listen to music).
A: I would, too.
OR I'd rather listen to music.

4

Pronunciation

Practice these conversations:

A: Do you like jazz?

B: Yes, I do.

C: I do, too. OR Really? I don't.

OR

A: Do you like jazz?

B: Not especially.

C: I don't either. OR Really? I do.

5

• **A, B** and **C,** ask each other about what you each like, and fill in this chart. Use a ✓ if your classmate likes something. Use an X, if he or she doesn't. Follow the example in Exercise 4.

	A	B	C
jazz			
classical music			
baseball			
westerns			

• Find a partner from a different group. Use the information above and have conversations like this about the people in your first group.

A: Would .... like to go to the jazz concert?
B: Probably. She likes jazz. Would .... like to go to the violin concert?
A: Probably not. He doesn't like classical music.

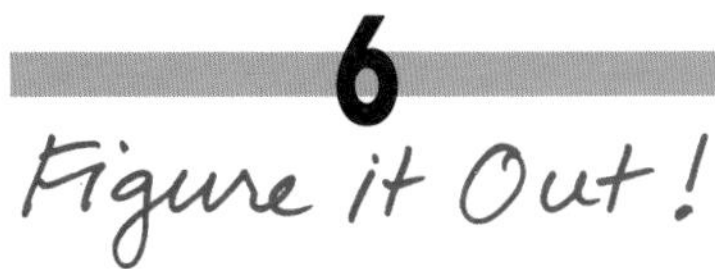

6

Figure it Out!

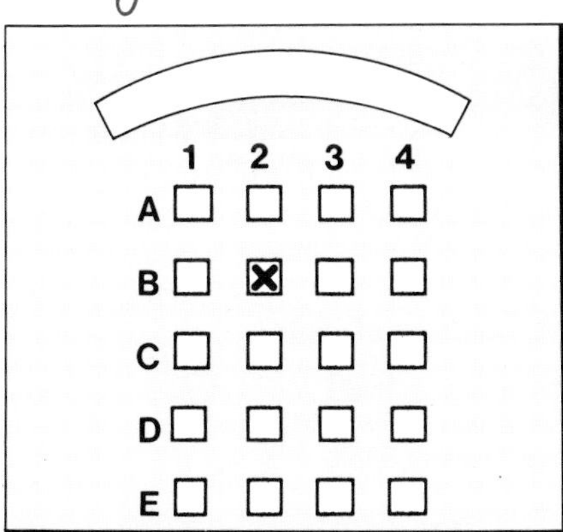

You have five tickets to the theater. Your seat number is B2. Your partner's (B's) seat is on your right. Your brother's seat is behind yours. Your sister's seat is on his left. Her husband's parents' seats are behind them. Figure out the seat numbers and tell your partner. Use *yours, his, hers* and *theirs.*

A: .... is yours.
B: Right. And your brother's?
A: .... is ....

7

Pronunciation

In words of two syllables, the stress is usually on the first syllable:

bóring

Sometimes it's on the second syllable:

yoursélf

Where's the stress in these words? Practice saying them after your teacher.

depressed	rather
different	Hello
ticket	maybe
foreign	evening
someday	

8

• **A,** ask questions. **B,** give true answers. Have conversations like this:

you visit Antarctica

A: Will you visit Antarctica someday?
B: I hope so. OR I hope not.

1. you visit Antarctica
2. there be peace in the world
3. we have another world war
4. people live to be 150
5. you be famous
6. I be very rich
7. ....

• Continue with conversations like this:

you'll drive across the U.S.

A: Do you think you'll drive across the United States someday?
B: Maybe someday. OR I doubt it.

1. you'll drive across the U.S.
2. people will live on the moon
3. you'll go to the North Pole
4. our English will be perfect
5. I'll be a movie star
6. ....

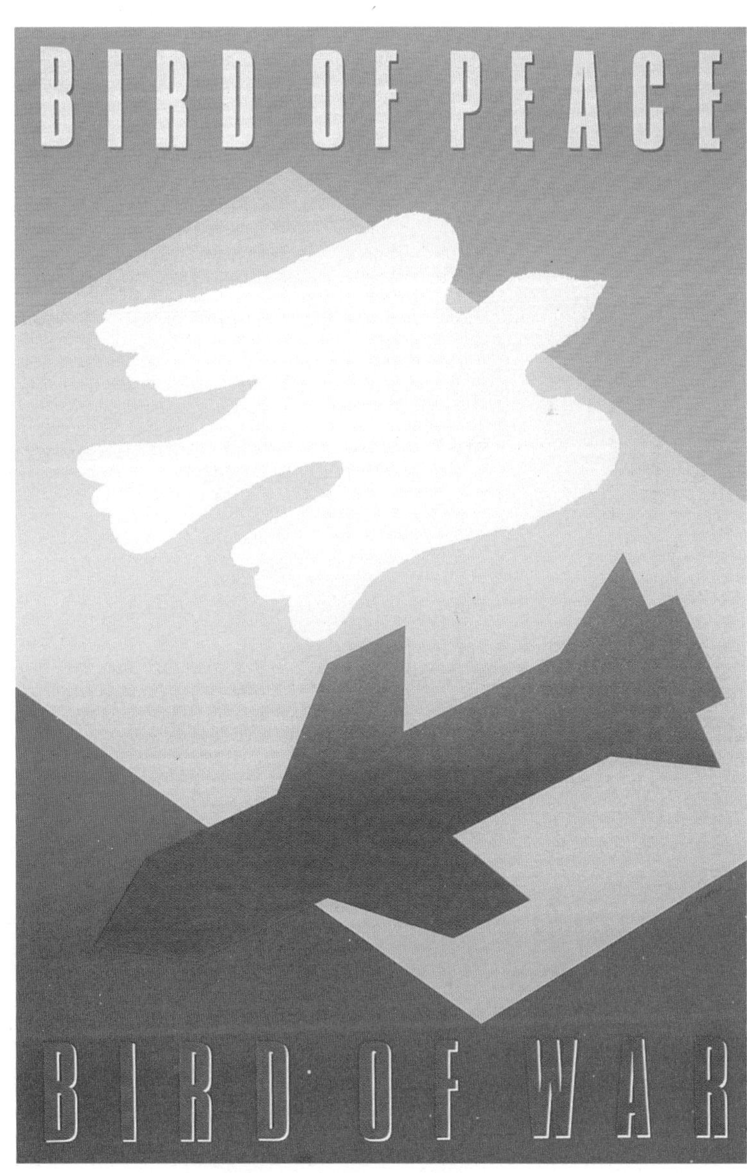

Mike Quon 1985

9
Culture Capsule

When television was new, only big cities in the United States had TV stations, or channels. Now almost everyone in the U.S. has a wide choice of channels. There are "regular" channels and cable channels. New York City, for example, has 7 regular channels. And one cable company there offers 34 more. Regular channels are free, but people pay for cable channels, usually every month.

These are some popular cable channels on American TV:

A&E Arts and Entertainment (plays, concerts, dance)
***CNN** Cable News Network
DIS The Disney Channel (for children)
ESN Eastern Sports Network
***HBO** Home Box Office (movies)
***TMC** The Movie Channel
***SHO** Showtime (movies)
MTV Music Television (popular music videos)

*24 hours a day

How many TV channels can you get in your town or city? Do you have to pay for the "regular" ones? Does your town or city have cable TV? What kinds of programs can you get on it?

Do you have a TV at home? Which American cable TV channels would you like to watch? What do you like to watch on TV?

10
Put It Together

- **A** and **B,** write a questionnaire to find out your classmates' likes and dislikes and hopes for the future. Below are some possible subjects and questions. For more ideas, see the questionnaire on the first page of this unit.

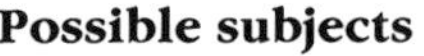

Possible subjects

music	food
sports	vacations
movies	TV

Possible questions

Who's/What's your favorite ....?
Do you like (to) ....?
Would you rather .... or ....?
Would you like to .... someday?

- Work with another pair of students (C and D). **A,** ask C the questions on your questionnaire. **C,** ask A. **B,** ask D. **D,** ask B.

I know how to . . .

CHECKLIST

USE THESE FORMS

☐ **Will**

I you he, she, it we they	will ('ll) will not (won't)

questions
Will your life be different in five years?
Where will you live?

short answers
Yes, it will. No, it won't.

statements
You'll be famous.
Maybe I'll have the same job.
I probably won't see Mt. Everest.

☐ **Embedded Questions**

Do you think + *Will you* eat out tonight?
Do you think *you will* eat out tonight?

☐ **Would Like To/Would Rather**

I you he, she, it we they	would ('d)

questions
Would you like to be famous?
Would you rather go out or watch TV?

short answers
Yes, I would. No, he wouldn't.

statements
I'd like to go to a concert.
He wouldn't like to go to a play.
I'd rather go out (than watch TV).

☐ **Possessive Pronouns**

mine, yours, his, hers, ours, theirs
Sean Connery's my favorite actor. Who's *yours?*
Mine's Woody Allen.

USE ENGLISH TO

☐ **talk about likes and dislikes**
Do you like to listen to music? What kind of music do you like?
I like jazz. I don't like popular music.

☐ **talk about desires**
What would you like to do for your next vacation?
I'd like to go to an exciting place.

☐ **talk about preferences**
Would you rather watch TV or go out?
I'd rather watch TV.

☐ **agree with someone**
I do, too./ I would, too./ I don't, either.

☐ **disagree with someone**
Really? I do/ don't/ would/ wouldn't.
I'd rather go out.

☐ **talk about future possibilities**
Do you think you'll go to the moon?
Probably (not)./ Maybe./ I doubt it.
I hope so/ not.

☐ **talk about these subjects**
hopes for the future favorites
entertainment sports music TV

☐ UNDERSTAND THESE EXPRESSIONS

Not especially.
You look (depressed).
You've got to have dreams.
Why do you say that?

eat out
fill out
go out

Listening

1

Listen to the questions. There are two correct answers for each question. Choose the one that gives **your** true opinion.

You will hear, "1. Do you like Walt Disney movies?"
The correct answer can be *a* or *b*.

1. a. Yes, I do.
   b. Not especially.
   c. Yes, I would.
   d. No, I wouldn't.
2. a. Yes, I do.
   b. Not especially.
   c. Yes, I would.
   d. No, I wouldn't.
3. a. Yes, I would.
   b. No, I wouldn't.
   c. I'd rather watch TV.
   d. I'd rather go out.
4. a. Yes, I would.
   b. No, I wouldn't.
   c. I hope so.
   d. I hope not.
5. a. Yes, I do.
   b. No, I don't.
   c. Probably.
   d. Probably not.
6. a. I hope so.
   b. I hope not.
   c. Yes, I would.
   d. No, I wouldn't.
7. a. I hope so.
   b. I hope not.
   c. Yes, I do.
   d. Not especially.
8. a. I'd rather play sports.
   b. I'd rather listen to music.
   c. Maybe someday.
   d. I doubt it.

2

WHAT ARE YOU LIKE?

Answer Yes or No

YES **1.** Do you like classical music better than jazz or rock?
YES **2.** Do you like to eat at foreign restaurants?
YES **3.** In general, would you rather go to a movie than a sports event?
YES **4.** Would you like to go to the moon someday?

This is part of a questionnaire that someone filled out. Listen to the radio ads. Would she like to attend the events they advertise? Check *Probably* or *Probably Not.*

	Probably	**Probably Not**
1.	☐	☐
2.	☐	☐
3.	☐	☐
4.	☐	☐
5.	☐	☐

3

You will hear people talk about their likes and dislikes. Choose the appropriate response for each.

1. a. It's mine, too.
   b. Really? I don't.
2. a. I don't, either.
   b. I do, too.
3. a. Mine is tennis.
   b. Probably.
4. a. I would, too.
   b. Really? I don't.
5. a. Really? I'd rather play sports.
   b. Really? I'd rather go to the movies.
6. a. Really? I do.
   b. Really? I don't.
7. a. Probably not.
   b. I would, too.

4

Give true answers.

1. ....
2. ....
3. ....
4. ....
5. ....
6. ....

Episode Twelve

Robert turns the lights on in his cabin and offers Christina a seat. "Make yourself comfortable. What would you like to drink?"

"Some cognac, please."

Robert gives Christina the drink and sits down next to her. "Now tell me more about the Moon of India."

"Why are you so interested in the Moon of India?"

"Don't you know?" Robert's voice is cold.

"No, I don't know. It's very strange. You're the second person. . . ."

"What did you say? Who's the other person?"

"It's not important, Robert. Aren't you going to make yourself a drink?"

"Don't play games with me, Christina. You know about the Moon of India. Who's the other person?"

"You're frightening me, Robert. What's the matter? I don't understand. I think I'd better leave."

Christina gets up and walks to the door. Robert moves in front of her.

"Robert, let me go."

"Where is the necklace?" Robert takes a gun from his pocket. "Where is the necklace?" he repeats.

"I don't know what you're talking about. You're crazy."

"So, it's the old lady. She found the necklace. Not you."

"What are you talking about?"

"I'm talking about the Moon of India. Your aunt has it and I'm going to get it from her. But you'll have to stay with me until I do."

In the Jordan's cabin, Agatha is explaining to Lucy what happened. They are looking at the picture.

"Yesterday, I found the necklace behind the painting. Tonight, when I returned from the ball, I found the painting on the floor."

Suddenly the phone rings.

"Agatha, this is Robert Grant. You have something I want. Bring the necklace to my cabin right away or you'll lose something very valuable. Here, listen."

"Agatha, it's me, Christina. Please do what he asks. He has a gun and he'll use it."

"You have ten minutes," says Robert.

"I'll need more time. The necklace is at the purser's. Give me twenty minutes."

"Twenty minutes and no more. And don't say a word to anyone." The phone cuts off.

Agatha turns to Lucy, "That was Robert. He stole the necklace. He's holding Christina as a hostage. If I don't give him the necklace, he's going to kill her."

Lucy takes Agatha's hand. "Don't worry. Follow my instructions and Christina won't get hurt."

Comprehension Check

1. Why does Robert ask Christina about the Moon of India?
2. What happens when Christina tries to leave the cabin?
3. How does Robert know that Agatha has the necklace?
4. On the phone, what does Robert tell Agatha to do?
5. Why does Agatha say she will do it?
6. Is Lucy going to help Agatha?

UNIT 13

Cathy: Would you like to come to dinner on Saturday, Jay?
Jay: I'd like to, Cathy, but I'm going to be out of town. Thanks for the invitation.
Cathy: Sure. We'll try again sometime.

Cathy: Are you going to be around for the weekend, Steve?
Steve: I probably will.
Cathy: Would you like to come to dinner at our house on Saturday?
Steve: Sure! That would be really nice.
Cathy: Great.
Steve: What time?
Cathy: Oh, about 6:00.
Steve: Thanks a lot, Cathy. I'll see you then.

Don: Come on in, Steve. Here, I'll take your coat.
Liz: Hi, Steve. I'm Cathy and Don's niece, Liz.
Steve: Hi, Liz. It's nice to meet you.
Cathy (from the kitchen): Make yourself comfortable, Steve. Dinner won't be ready for a while.

Don: Cathy, could you pass the potatoes, please? . . . Thanks.
Cathy: Would anyone like anything else? More meat? Vegetables?
Liz: Nothing for me, thanks. I'm saving room for dessert.
Steve: I'll have some more meat. It's delicious. I always have room for dessert.

(later) . . .
Cathy: Would you like some pie? We have apple and peach.
Steve: Yes, thank you. Could I have a little of each?

Steve: Thank you very much. It was a wonderful dinner, and I enjoyed the company.
Don and Cathy: We enjoyed it, too. Come again!
Liz: It was nice meeting you, Steve.
All: Good night.

Speaking

1

Fill in the blanks with *will, (')ll, would, (')d* or *could,* and practice the conversations.

1. A: .... you like to go to a movie with us tonight?
   B: I'.................... like to, but I can't. Thanks for the invitation.
   A: Sure. We'.................... try again sometime.
2. A: .... anyone like anything else?
   B: I'.................... have some more potatoes, please.
3. A: I'.................... help you with that.
   B: Thank you.
4. A: Are you going to be around this weekend?
   B: I probably ....
   A: .... you give me some help with my car on Saturday?
   B: OK. About 2:00?
   A: Fine. I'.................... see you then.

2
Pronunciation

In words of three syllables, the stress is usually on the first or second syllable (Saturday, November).

Where's the stress in these words? Practice saying them.

anything	restaurant
tomato	customer
probably	celebrate
important	holiday
potatoes	vegetable
together	November

3

Event

dinner
a party
a barbecue

Day

Saturday
New Year's Eve
the Fourth of July
Thanksgiving

Time

6:00
8:00
noon
1:00

Reason

visit my parents
be out of town/be away
have out-of-town guests

A, invite your partner to your house. Choose an event and a day from the suggestions above. **B,** respond to A's invitation. If you can't come, give a reason. **A,** if B can come, set a time. Have conversations like these:

A: Would you like to come to dinner on Saturday?
B: Sure! That would be really nice.
A: Great.
B: What time?
A: Oh, about 6:00.
B: Thanks a lot. I'll see you then.

OR

A: Would you like to come to dinner on Saturday?
B: I'd like to, but I'm going to visit my parents that day. Thanks for the invitation.
A: Sure. We'll try again sometime.

4

1. bring you some aspirin

2. mail that for you

3. help you pick those up

4. open that for you

5. get those down for you

6. help you with those

- **A,** choose a picture (1, 3 or 5) and act out what's happening. **B,** find the picture A is acting out and offer to help. **A,** thank B.

A: (acts out picture #5)
B: I'll get those down for you.
A: Thank you.

- **B,** choose a picture (2, 4 or 6) and act it out. **A,** offer to help.

- **B,** this time, ask your partner to help you. **A,** agree to help. Change *you* to *me, that* to *this* and *those* to *these.*

B: (acts out picture #4) Could you open this for me, please?
A: Sure, I'd be glad to.

5

You want to go to some of these restaurants. Ask your partner about them.

A: Do I have to make a reservation at .... ?
B: Yes, you do. OR No, you don't.
A: Do I have to dress up?
B: Well, men have to wear jackets and ties.
OR No, you don't. It's informal.
A: Can I pay by credit card?
B: Yes, you can.
OR They don't accept credit cards.

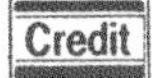 Reservations are necessary.

 Men must wear jackets and ties.

Credit — The restaurant accepts most credit cards.

$ — No credit cards. Cash only.

A

1. Ask B about some of these restaurants:

The Hunan Palace
The Jade Garden
The Little Chef
The Acropolis
Spiro's

2. Answer B's questions. Use this guide:

	Reservations	Jackets and ties	Credit	$
Buckley's		●		●
Caesar's	●		●	
Atlantic Sushi				●
Little Tokyo			●	
Manuel's	●	●		●

B

1. Answer A's questions. Use this guide:

	Reservations	Jackets and ties	Credit	$
Hunan Palace	●	●		●
The Jade Garden			●	
The Little Chef			●	
The Acropolis			●	
Spiro's		●		●

2. Ask A about some of these restaurants:

Buckley's
Caesar's
Atlantic Sushi
Little Tokyo
Manuel's

6

A and **B,** you're having dinner at Buckley's. Look at the menu. Decide what you want to order. Ask your partner about his or her choices.

A: What're you going to have?
B: I'm going to have the sirloin steak.
OR I'm not sure. I'll probably have the sirloin steak. What about you?
A: I ....
B: Are you going to have an appetizer?

BUCKLEY'S

Menu

Entrees

broiled lobster	$15.95
lamb chops	$14.75
New York sirloin steak	$12.95
prime rib of beef	$13.95
lemon baked chicken	$11.50

All entrees include choice of potato, vegetable, and salad bar.

Appetizers

shrimp cocktail	$5.95
fruit cup	$2.50
tomato or grapefruit juice	$1.25
soup of the day	$2.50

Desserts

Ask to see our dessert menu.

7

A, you're the waiter or waitress. **B** and **C,** you're customers at the restaurant.

A: Are you ready to order?
B: Yes, I'll have the ....
A: How would you like your ....? Rare, medium or well done?
B: ...., please.
A: Would you like an appetizer?
B: Yes, I'd like the ....
OR No, thank you.
A: What kind of .... would you like? We have ....
B: ...., please.
A: Thank you. You can help yourself to the salad bar anytime.

(later) . . .

A: Would you like anything else?
B: Yes, could you bring us your dessert menu? And I'd like some more coffee, please.
C: Certainly.

8

Culture Capsule

Thanksgiving is an important holiday in the United States. It's a special time when friends and family get together and share a meal. The meal usually includes roast turkey, stuffing, cranberry sauce, sweet potatoes, mashed potatoes, squash and other vegetables, and pumpkin and apple pies.

The first Thanksgiving was in 1621. Native Americans and early settlers from Europe shared a meal after a very difficult winter. They gave thanks for food and for life itself.

Americans now celebrate Thanksgiving on the fourth Thursday in November.

What's an important holiday in your country? When is it? How did it begin? Is there a special meal? What is it? Does everyone celebrate this holiday?

9

Put It Together

Plan a special holiday dinner with your partner. Decide: When will it be? What will you eat?

Invite another pair of students to join you. Greet them when they arrive. Make them feel welcome.

A, B, C and **D,** now you're eating dinner. **A** and **B,** offer food. **C** and **D,** make requests for different dishes.

C and **D,** thank A and B, and say good night.

I know how to . . .

USE THESE FORMS

☐ **Will**

for talking about the future with the verb be
I'll be out of town on Saturday.
Dinner won't be ready for a while.

for promising
We'll try again sometime.

for offering to help
I'll take your coat.

for deciding
I'll have some more meat.

☐ **Will vs. Going To**

When plans are definite, going to *is usually used.*
I'm going to have the steak.
(That's my final decision.)

When there is some uncertainty, will *is usually used with words like* probably *and* maybe.
I'll probably have the steak.
(I probably will, but maybe I won't.)

When the verb is be, *either* will *or* going to *can be used for definite future plans.*
I'll be out of town on Saturday.
I'm going to be out of town on Saturday.

USE ENGLISH TO

☐ **invite someone**
Would you like to come to dinner on Thanksgiving?

☐ **accept an invitation**
Sure! That would be really nice.

☐ **decline an invitation**
I'd like to, but I'm going to be out of town.
Thanks for the invitation.

☐ **welcome someone**
Come on in. Make yourself comfortable.

☐ **offer help**
I'll take your coat.

☐ **offer food**
Would you like anything else?

☐ **accept an offer of food**
I'd like some more coffee, please.
I'll have some more meat.

☐ **decline an offer of food**
No, nothing for me, thanks.

☐ **make a request**
Could I have a little of each?
Could you give me some help with my car?

☐ **order in a restaurant**
I'll have/I'd like the steak.
How would you like your. . . ?
Medium, please.

☐ **talk about these subjects**
holidays food
dinner at someone's house
restaurants menus

☐ UNDERSTAND THESE EXPRESSIONS

Cash only.
Certainly. (formal)
Come again!
Good night.
Help yourself.
It was nice meeting you.
No credit cards.
Pass (the potatoes), please.
Sure.

be out of town
be around for (the weekend)
dress up
make a reservation
pay by credit card

CHECKLIST

Listening

1

Choose the appropriate response to each speaker you hear. Number the responses 1, 2, 3 or 4 in each part.

Part 1:

__ a. Sure. We'll try again soon.

__ b. Sure! That would be really nice.

__ c. Would you like to come to our house for dinner?

__ d. I probably will.

Part 2:

__ a. Thank you.

__ b. Yes, I'll have the prime rib, please.

__ c. Nothing more for me, thanks.

__ d. Sure. I'd be glad to.

2

Match the speakers and the situations. In each part, number the situations 1, 2, 3 or 4.

Part 1: The speaker is:

__ a. ordering in a restaurant

__ b. asking for help

__ c. agreeing to help

__ d. offering help

Part 2: The speaker is:

__ a. inviting someone

__ b. declining an invitation

__ c. offering food

__ d. refusing food

3

Some of these conversations take place in someone's house. Others take place in a restaurant. Put a check in the correct column.

	House	Restaurant
1.	☐	☐
2.	☐	☐
3.	☐	☐
4.	☐	☐
5.	☐	☐
6.	☐	☐
7.	☐	☐

4

Write appropriate responses.

1. ....
2. ....
3. ....
4. ....
5. ....
6. ....

Episode Thirteen

Agatha knocks at Robert's door. The door opens and Agatha sees Christina tied to a chair. Robert closes the door quickly. "Where is it?" he demands.

Agatha gives him the necklace. He looks at it and puts it in his jacket pocket.

"Thank you, Agatha. Sorry about this." He ties Agatha up next to Christina. Then he makes a telephone call. "Could you get a taxi for me first thing this morning? Yes, it's Grant. Robert Grant. I have a very important business meeting. Thank you." He puts the phone down, puts his jacket on and points the gun at the two women. "And now I have to say goodbye to you two ladies." He laughs, puts the gun in his pocket and leaves the cabin.

The ship is in port at Malaga. Robert is walking along the deck, looking for the taxi. He sees a man following him. He goes up to another deck. He sees a second man watching him. He starts to run, but the men follow him up and down and across the ship. Robert keeps running. Then he hears a familiar voice. "Stop, Robert." He turns around. Lucy is pointing a gun at him. "So you're a cop," he says.

"Give me the necklace," Lucy replies. He pulls out the necklace and starts to give it to her. Suddenly, he knocks her gun to the ground and grabs her.

"C'mon officer, you're going to help me get off this ship."

They walk to the gangway. The two men, who are Interpol agents, come closer.

"Get back or I'll kill her."

"Do as he says. He has a gun."

When they reach the gangway, there is a group of people waiting to go down. Frank is among them.

"Robert, Lucy, this is a surprise. I didn't know you were. . . ."

"Shut up, Frank," says Robert and shows him the gun.

"Go away, Frank," advises Lucy.

"Lucy, let me help you. . . ." And Frank takes a step towards her.

Robert moves toward Frank and Lucy tries to get Robert's gun. There is a fight and the gun falls to the deck below. Robert looks down for

his gun, and the necklace falls out of his pocket. It falls on the tray of a man selling souvenirs on the dock below. The Interpol agents grab Robert.

Lucy runs down the gangway to get the necklace but the crowds leaving the ship get in her way. The man selling souvenirs, with the real Moon of India on his tray, walks away from the ship. Lucy runs after him.

Comprehension Check

1. Why does Robert tie up Christina and Agatha?
2. Two men are following Robert. Who are they?
3. Does Lucy take the necklace from Robert?
4. Who tries to help Lucy?
5. What happens to the necklace?
6. Do the police catch Robert?

UNIT 14

Herb: There aren't any interesting programs on TV tonight. Do you want to play a game?
Judy: Sure. How about "Do You Know?"?
Herb: All right, but you always win.
Judy: I know. That's why I like it.

Herb: "What's the smallest dog?"
Judy: I'm not sure. It can't be the St. Bernard! It might be the Pekingese. I know! It must be the Chihuahua.
Herb: I think you're right. Let me see. Yes, it's the Chihuahua.

Judy: "Is the Earth getting warmer or cooler?"
Herb: I don't know. I'll say *cooler*.
Judy: I think it's getting warmer. Yes, I'm right.
Herb: You're always right . . . . I'm going to get a Coke. Do you want one?
Judy: Sure.

Herb: Whose turn is it?
Judy: It's your turn to ask a question. It's my turn to answer.
Herb: "Who ran the first four-minute mile?"
Judy: Oh, what was his name? He was British, wasn't he? Roger something. Roger Bannister. He did it in the early '50s. 1954?
Herb: "Roger Bannister, in 1954." See? You're never wrong!

Judy: "Where are the next Summer Olympics going to be?"
Herb: Whose Coke is this?
Judy: It must be yours. I finished mine. Are you going to answer your question?
Herb: I will in a minute. I'm thinking, I'm thinking.

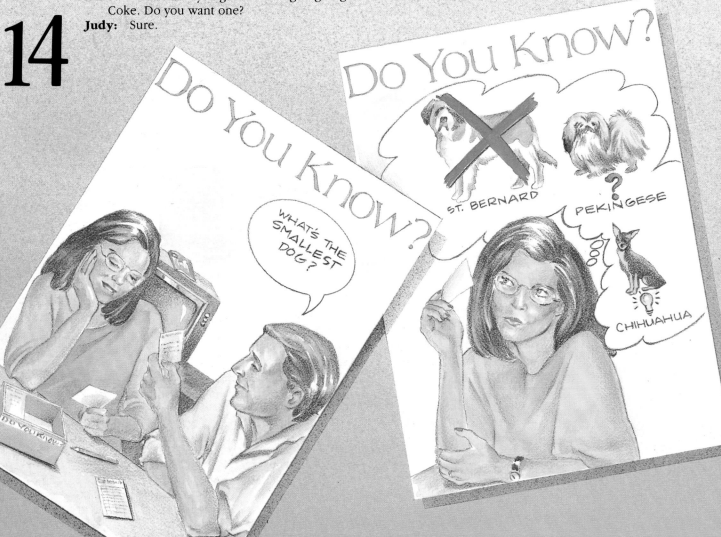

Speaking

1

Ask and answer the questions on Herb's and Judy's cards. Have conversations like these:

A: What's the smallest dog?
B: The Chihuahua.
OR I'm not sure. I think it's the Chihuahua.
A: You're right.

OR A: What's the smallest dog?
B: I don't know.
A: It's the Chihuahua.

OR A: What's the smallest dog?
B: Is it the Pekingese?
A: No, it's the Chihuahua.

A

1. Ask B questions 2, 3 and 5 on Herb's card.

DO YOU KNOW?

- **1.** What's the smallest dog?
- **2.** Where do people use yen for money?
- **3.** Are the world's oceans getting bigger or smaller?
- **4.** Who ran the first four-minute mile?
- **5.** When is Halley's Comet going to come again?

Answers: 2. in Japan
3. bigger
5. in 2060

2. Try to answer B's questions.

B

1. Try to answer A's questions:

2. Ask A questions 1, 2 and 4 on Judy's card.

DO YOU KNOW?

- **1.** Where's the Taj Mahal?
- **2.** What country has the biggest population?
- **3.** Is the Earth getting warmer or cooler?
- **4.** Who invented the telephone?
- **5.** Where are the next Summer Olympics going to be?

Answers 1. in India
2. the People's Republic of China
4. Alexander Graham Bell (Canadian)

2

Pronunciation

Practice saying these sentences with your partner. Match questions with answers.

1. What's the smallest dog?
2. Is the Earth getting warmer or cooler?
3. Whose turn is it?
4. Whose Coke is this?

a. It must be yours. I finished mine.
b. It can't be the St. Bernard. It must be the Pekingese.
c. It's your turn to ask a question. It's my turn to answer.
d. I'll say cooler.

3

Have conversations like this. Use *can't, might* and *must.*

A: (points to women's shoes) Whose are these?
B: They can't be Van's. They might be Alexandra's or Ryuko's. (points to biggest belt) Whose is this?
A: It must be Van's.

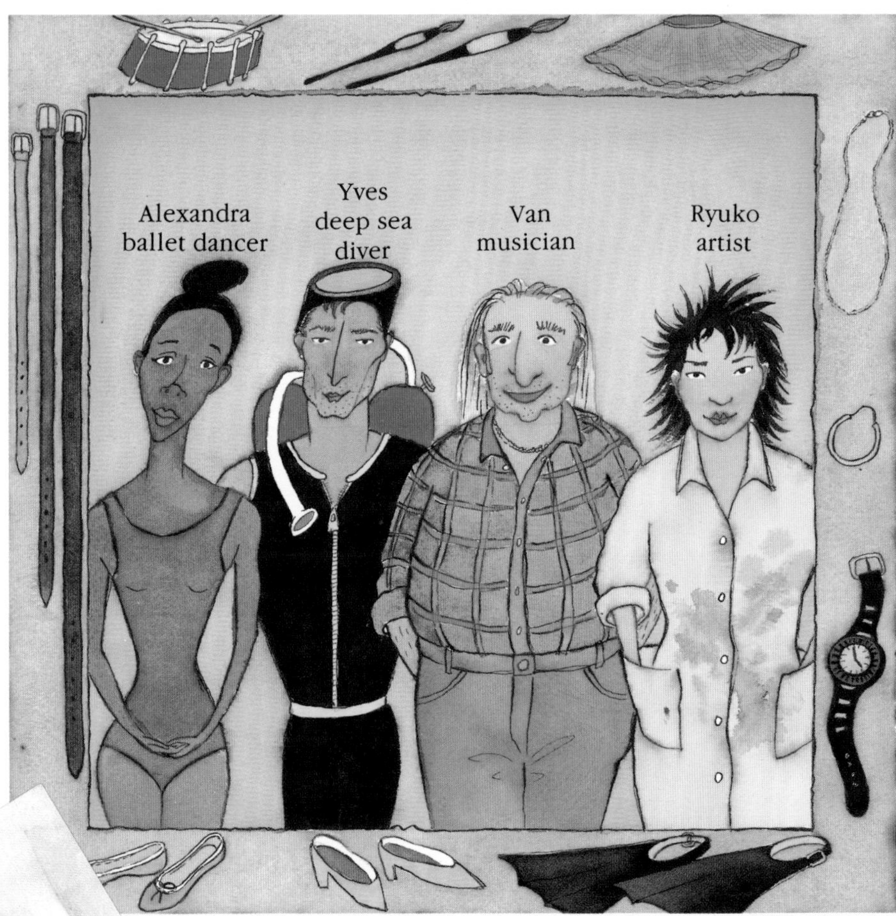

4

- You and your partner are good friends. Invite him or her to:

play cards go to a movie go out for pizza	tonight

A: Do you want to .... ?
B: Sure. Sounds good.
OR Sorry, I can't. I have to do my homework.

- You and your partner don't know each other very well. Invite him or her to:

play tennis go jogging have lunch together	tomorrow afternoon

B: Would you like to .... ?
A: Thanks. I'd like that.
OR I'm sorry, I can't, but thanks for the invitation.

5

- You and your partner are good friends. You're at your house.

Offer A: a Coke
a piece of cake
a glass of milk

B: I'm going to get .... (Do you) want one?
A: Sure.
OR No, thanks.

- You and your partner don't know each other very well. You're at your house.

Offer B: a cup of coffee
some cookies
some fruit

A: Would you like .... ?
B: Yes, please.
OR Nothing for me, thank you.

6

When you think something is true, but you're not completely sure, you can say it like this:	When you think something is not true, but you're not completely sure, you can say it like this:
affirmative statement — *negative tag question*	*negative statement* — *affirmative tag question*
He was English, wasn't he?	He wasn't French, was he?

- Practice saying these sentences. Notice how the tag questions change.

1a. The Chihuaha is the smallest dog, isn't it?
b. The Pekingese isn't the smallest dog, is it?
2a. There are five questions on Judy's card, aren't there?
b. There aren't any good TV programs tonight, are there?
3a. The questions are difficult, aren't they?
b. The questions aren't easy, are they?
4a. Herb was right, wasn't he?
b. Judy wasn't sure, was she?
5a. Judy will win the game, won't she?
b. Herb won't win the game, will he?
6a. Four people can play, can't they?
b. Eight people can't play, can they?

- Are these statements true or false? Have conversations like these:

There are 50 states in the U.S.

A: There are 50 states in the U.S., aren't there?
B: Yes, there are.

OR

A: There aren't 50 states in the U.S., are there?
B: Yes, there are.

Texas is the biggest state.

A: Texas is the biggest state, isn't it?
B: No, it isn't. Alaska is.

OR

A: Texas isn't the biggest state, is it?
B: No, it isn't. Alaska is.

1. There are 50 states in the U.S.
2. Texas is the biggest state.
3. George Washington was the first president of the U.S.
4. There's a presidential election every two years.
5. Women can be president.
6. There will be a presidential election in 1996.
7. There are a lot of Japanese cherry trees in Washington, D.C.
8. Rhode Island is the smallest state.
9. California and Oregon are on the Pacific Coast.
10. John Kennedy was the youngest president.
11. People can be president for more than eight years.
12. There will be a presidential election in 1994.

A

1. Use tag questions to tell B what you think about statements 1–6 above.
2. Listen to B and say if he or she is right or wrong. Answers: 7. T 8. T 9. T 10. T 11. F 12. F

B

1. Listen to A and say if he or she is right or wrong. Answers: 1. T 2. F (Alaska is) 3. T 4. F 5. T 6. T
2. Use tag questions to tell A what you think about statements 7–12 above.

- **A,** ask B five real questions using question tags. **B,** answer with true information. For example, A: *You're studying Russian, aren't you?* B: *No, I'm not.*

7
Culture Capsule

Chess

Scrabble   Gin

Scrabble is a word game. Each player gets seven letters and has to make words. The letters have different points and the player with the most points wins.

Gin is a card game. Each player gets ten cards and has to match them in groups of three and four.

Chess is a game for two players. Each player has sixteen pieces on a board with sixty-four squares.

Do people in your country play these games? Do you know how to play these games? What (other) games can you play? Which ones do you like the best?

8

Use your own ideas to fill in the information about Mata Kira. Have conversations like this:

A: How old is she?
B: I think she's 25. What do you think?
A: I think so too.

OR

A: How old is she?
B: I think she's 25.
A: Really? I don't think so. I think she's 40.

Name *Mata Kira*
Age ____
Marital status ____
Children ____
Occupation ____
Place of birth ____
Languages ____
Home city ____
Habits *Usually gets up at 6 AM*
Dislikes ____

9
Guess Who!

What do you know about the other people in your class? Make statements about one person until your partner guesses who it is. Use the ideas below.

A: She's from Tokyo and she likes jazz.
B: Is it Yoko?
A: No, it isn't. She's wearing a white sweater.
B: Is it Sumi?
A: No. She went to California last year.
B: Oh, it must be Kimiko.
A: Right!

Ideas

1. likes/doesn't like tennis, movies, Indian food, sports cars
2. plays the violin, piano, drums
3. has long hair, short hair, curly hair
4. moved/went to .... last week, month, year
5. is going to get married/study computer science next year
6. will probably be a famous .... someday

10
Put It Together

Ask about your partner's ideas for his/her future.

A: What are you going to do after this course/this summer/next year?
B: .... How about you?
A: ....
B: Would you like to .... in the future?
A: .... What about you?
B: ....
A: Will you ever .... ?
B: ....

Some Ideas

take a long vacation
write a book
travel
study (Russian)
be (an astronaut)

I know how to . . .

CHECKLIST

USE THESE FORMS

☐ **Might/Can't/Must**

Might *expresses possibility.*
It might be the Pekingese.

Can't *expresses impossibility.*
It can't be the St. Bernard.

Must *expresses probability.*
It must be the Chihuahua.

☐ **Whose**

Whose	turn	is	it	?
	Coke		this	

☐ **Tag Questions**

affirmative statement — *negative tag*

You're studying English, aren't you?
Alaska is the biggest state in the U.S., isn't it?
There are fifty states, aren't there?
Women can be president, can't they?
There will be a presidential election in 1996, won't there?

negative statement — *affirmative tag*

You're not studying Russian, are you?
Texas isn't the biggest state anymore, is it?
There aren't fifty-one states, are there?
People can't be president for more than eight years, can they?
There won't be an election in 1995, will there?

USE ENGLISH TO

☐ **invite someone to do something—informally**
Do you want to play cards tonight?
Sure. Sounds good.
Sorry, I can't. I have to . . . .

☐ **and more formally**
Would you like to play tennis tomorrow?
Thanks. I'd like that.
I'm sorry, I can't, but thanks for the invitation.

☐ **offer something—informally**
I'm going to get a Coke. (Do you) want one?
Sure./No, thanks.

☐ **and more formally**
Would you like some fruit?
Yes, please./Nothing for me, thanks.

☐ **express uncertainty**
I'm not sure.

☐ **talk about these subjects**
games   future plans

☐ UNDERSTAND THESE EXPRESSIONS

All right.
I'm not sure.
It's (your) turn.

get something (a soda)
get warmer/cooler
play a game
play cards

Listening

1

Part 1: You will hear six people speak. Match each one with the correct picture. Write the number of the speaker in the box.

Part 2: Listen again to the tape. From the list, choose the best response for each item you hear. Write its letter in the blank.

1. ___
2. ___
3. ___
4. ___
5. ___
6. ___

a. Hello, this is Chuck Wick. Is Marta there?
b. Hi! Come on in!
c. How do you do?
d. I'm sorry, I can't, But thanks for the invitation.
e. It depends. How much is it?
f. No, thank you. I'm just looking.
g. Really?
h. Same here. Take it easy.
i. Sure. Here it is.
j. Yes, some. How much do you need?
k. You're welcome.
l. Whose is that?

2

Are these conversations between friends or strangers? Check the correct column.

	Friends	Strangers
1.	☐	☐
2.	☐	☐
3.	☐	☐
4.	☐	☐
5.	☐	☐
6.	☐	☐
7.	☐	☐
8.	☐	☐
9.	☐	☐
10.	☐	☐

3

Here are some questions from earlier units. Give true answers.

1. ....
2. ....
3. ....
4. ....
5. ....
6. ....
7. ....
8. ....
9. ....
10. ....

Episode Fourteen

At the City Museum in New York, the director of the museum, Alexander Gray, is giving a press conference. Lieutenant Washington is with him. "The Moon of India is back home. The police have done an incredible job. Robert Grant, the man who stole the Moon of India and killed his partner is in jail. I would like to thank the police and one officer in particular, officer Lucy Cardozo. She caught Robert Grant and returned the Moon of India to us. Officer Cardozo is not with us today. But we, the people of this city, and especially the staff of this museum, thank her for a job well done."

At a party on the ship, Lucy, Frank, Christina and Agatha are talking.

"Why did he hide the necklace in our room?" asks Christina.

"He knew the police thought that the Moon of India was on the ship because of Paul Richardson's last words," explains Lucy, "and if they found the necklace in your room, they might think you stole it."

"Of course, I work at the museum, so they might suspect me."

"He planned to sell the necklace to a buyer in Marseilles, but he changed his plans because he was worried. I searched his room the night before. He knew somebody searched his room, but he didn't know who it was. In Barcelona, we followed him. We knew he had to sell the necklace, and we wanted him to take us to his buyer."

"Good thinking," says Agatha.

"You know the rest of the story," Lucy continues. "Agatha found the necklace. Robert came back to get it, and when he found it wasn't there, he used Christina as a hostage. But Agatha and I had a plan, and with the help of two Interpol agents, we caught him."

"When did the Interpol agents get on the ship?" asks Frank.

"We sent a message to Interpol after Robert called Agatha. They came on board the ship as soon as it docked in Malaga."

"And the buyer?" asks Frank.

"We've arrested him, too," says Lucy.

"There is one thing I would like to ask you, Frank," says Christina.

"Sure."

"Did you know that the Moon of India was on the ship?"

"No."

"Did you know that Lucy was a police officer?"

"No."

"I don't understand. The mystery story you're writing is so similar to what really happened."

"I can't explain it. Maybe I should be a detective."

"Take my place," says Lucy. "I need a vacation."

"Moon of India, get your Moon of India necklaces. One for nine dollars, two for fifteen. A steal at the price."

Comprehension Check

1. Who does Alexander Gray thank at the press conference? Why?
2. How did Robert Grant know the police suspected him?
3. Why did Robert Grant think the police would suspect Christina?
4. Why did Robert Grant use Christina as a hostage?
5. Did the police catch the buyer?
6. Why does Lucy think Frank knew about the Moon of India?

Word List

This word list contains both the active and receptive words on the first seven pages of each unit of the Student Book. The list does not include words which occur only in *The Moon of India* or the names of people and geographical locations. The page numbers next to each word indicate where it occurs for the first time. In cases where the same word is used with two different meanings, the page where each meaning first occurs is given.

A

B

C

U

V

W

Y

Irregular Verbs: Past Tense

be	was, were
begin	began
bring	brought
buy	bought
catch	caught
choose	chose
come	came
cost	cost
do	did
drive	drove
eat	ate
fall	fell
feel	felt
find	found
fly	flew
forget	forgot
get	got
give	gave
go	went
grow	grew
have	had
hear	heard
hide	hid
hold	held
know	knew
leave	left
lose	lost
make	made
mean	meant
meet	met
put	put
read	read
ring	rang
run	ran
say	said
see	saw
sell	sold
shake	shook
sing	sang
sit	sat
speak	spoke
spend	spent
steal	stole
swim	swam
take	took
teach	taught
tell	told
think	thought
understand	understood
wear	wore
write	wrote

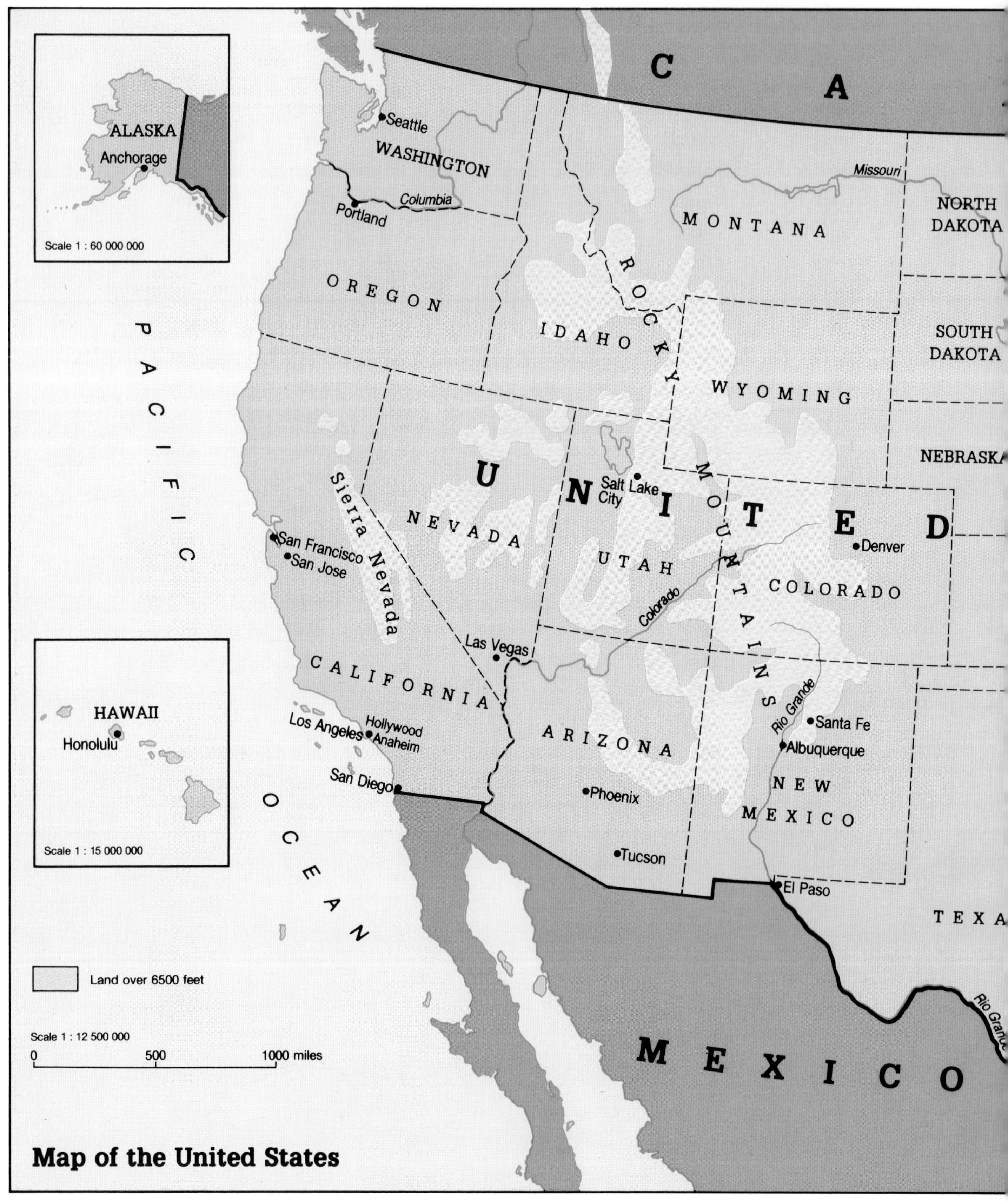
ALASKA
Anchorage
Scale 1 : 60 000 000
HAWAII
Honolulu
Scale 1 : 15 000 000
Land over 6500 feet
Scale 1 : 12 500 000
0
500
1000 miles
PACIFIC
OCEAN
CANADA
UNITED
MEXICO
Seattle
WASHINGTON
Columbia
Portland
OREGON
IDAHO
MONTANA
Missouri
NORTH DAKOTA
SOUTH DAKOTA
WYOMING
NEBRASKA
ROCKY MOUNTAINS
Salt Lake City
UTAH
NEVADA
Sierra Nevada
San Francisco
San Jose
CALIFORNIA
Las Vegas
Colorado
COLORADO
Denver
Los Angeles
Hollywood
Anaheim
San Diego
ARIZONA
Phoenix
Tucson
Rio Grande
Santa Fe
Albuquerque
NEW MEXICO
El Paso
TEXA

Map of the United States

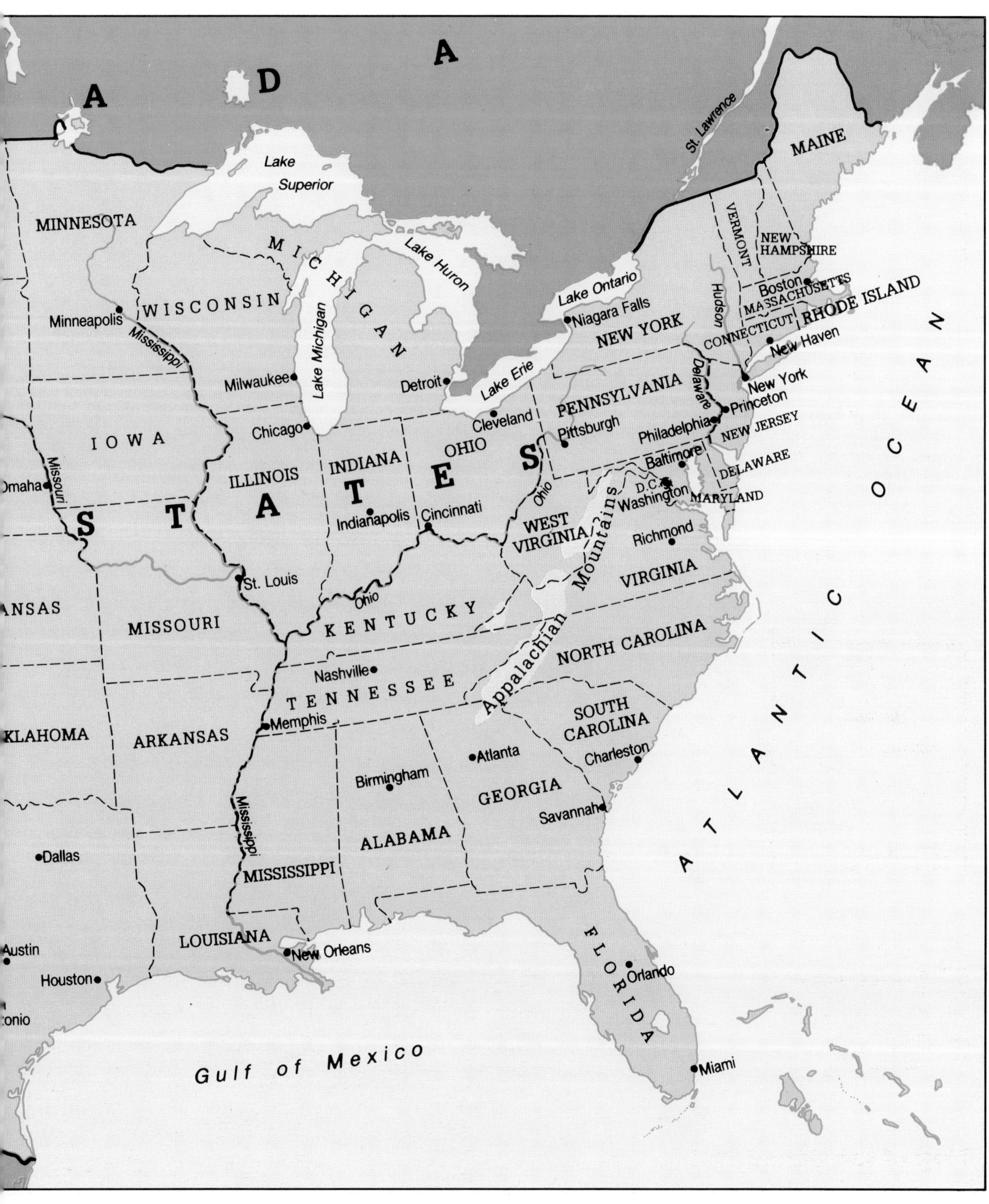
A
D
A
Lake
Superior
MINNESOTA
MICHIGAN
Lake Huron
St. Lawrence
MAINE
VERMONT
NEW HAMPSHIRE
WISCONSIN
Minneapolis
Mississippi
Lake Michigan
Milwaukee
Detroit
Lake Ontario
Niagara Falls
NEW YORK
Hudson
Boston
MASSACHUSETTS
RHODE ISLAND
CONNECTICUT
New Haven
New York
Delaware
Lake Erie
Cleveland
PENNSYLVANIA
Princeton
Philadelphia
NEW JERSEY
Pittsburgh
IOWA
Chicago
Omaha
Missouri
ILLINOIS
INDIANA
OHIO
S T A T E S
Baltimore
DELAWARE
D.C.
Washington
MARYLAND
Ohio
Indianapolis
Cincinnati
WEST VIRGINIA
Richmond
Mountains
Appalachian
St. Louis
VIRGINIA
ANSAS
MISSOURI
Ohio
KENTUCKY
NORTH CAROLINA
Nashville
TENNESSEE
SOUTH CAROLINA
KLAHOMA
ARKANSAS
Memphis
Atlanta
Charleston
Birmingham
GEORGIA
Savannah
Mississippi
ALABAMA
Dallas
MISSISSIPPI
ATLANTIC OCEAN
LOUISIANA
New Orleans
Austin
Houston
FLORIDA
Orlando
Miami
Gulf of Mexico